Contents Table

Section 7: Integrations and Extensions

Section 8: Project Planning Essentials

Section 9: Effective Collaboration Strategies

Section 10: Advanced Workflows and Automations

Section 11: Best Practices and Troubleshooting

Section 12: Real-World Applications

Section 13: The Road Ahead

Appendices

- **Appendix A: Glossary of Smartsheet Terms**
- **Appendix B: Resource Links and Reference Materials**
- **Appendix C: Smartsheet Keyboard Shortcuts**

~ Conclusion

Welcome & What You'll Learn

Welcome to **"Smartsheet Strategies: Driving Project Success"**! This book is your comprehensive guide to mastering Smartsheet, a powerful tool for project management, planning, tracking, and reporting. Whether you're a beginner looking to explore the basics or an experienced professional aiming to optimize your workflows, this book will help you harness Smartsheet's full potential to drive success in your projects.

Why Smartsheet?

Smartsheet has become a go-to solution for businesses and teams worldwide due to its versatility, ease of use, and robust features. It combines the familiarity of spreadsheets with advanced project management capabilities, enabling teams to plan, track, automate, and report on work seamlessly. With Smartsheet, you can:

- **Improve Collaboration**: Work in real time with your team, regardless of location.
- **Enhance Visibility**: Track progress, manage resources, and align stakeholders with interactive dashboards and reports.
- **Boost Efficiency**: Automate repetitive tasks and set up workflows to save time.
- **Streamline Decision-Making**: Use data-driven insights to make informed decisions.

What You'll Learn

This book is designed to guide you step-by-step through Smartsheet's features and capabilities, from the basics to advanced functionalities. Here's what you can expect to learn:

1. Master the Fundamentals

We'll start with an introduction to Smartsheet, its core concepts, and the basics of setting up your account and navigating the interface. This foundation will help you feel confident as you dive into the tool's capabilities.

2. Build and Customize Your Sheets

You'll learn how to create sheets from scratch or work with templates. Discover how to customize columns, rows, and cell properties to tailor your sheets to specific project needs.

3. Collaborate Effectively

Collaboration is at the heart of Smartsheet. Explore techniques for inviting team members, managing permissions, and sharing work seamlessly. We'll also cover best practices for version control and real-time communication.

4. Manage Projects and Tasks Like a Pro

From task creation and prioritization to Gantt chart visualization and automation, you'll gain the skills needed to efficiently manage timelines, dependencies, and milestones within Smartsheet.

5. Leverage Advanced Features

Dive deeper into Smartsheet's advanced functionalities, including formulas, conditional formatting, linking data across sheets, and creating automated workflows to streamline complex processes.

6. Analyze and Report with Confidence

Learn to build detailed reports, interactive dashboards, and key performance indicator (KPI) trackers. We'll guide you through exporting and sharing insights with stakeholders to drive transparency and accountability.

7. Explore Integrations and Innovations

Discover how to connect Smartsheet with third-party tools, use mobile apps for on-the-go management, and leverage Smartsheet Labs for creative solutions.

8. Optimize Project Planning

Gain insights into defining scope, aligning teams, managing resources, and mitigating risks—all within the Smartsheet platform.

9. Implement Effective Collaboration Strategies

Understand how to streamline communication, manage remote teams, and integrate Agile methodologies for dynamic project environments.

10. Embrace Automation and Workflows

Uncover the power of automation to create efficient, scalable processes. Learn to design complex workflows and use forms for seamless data collection.

11. Adopt Best Practices

We'll share proven strategies for standardizing templates, maintaining data security, and troubleshooting common issues.

12. Learn from Real-World Applications

Explore case studies showcasing how Smartsheet is used in diverse industries, from marketing to IT, event planning, and beyond.

13. Prepare for the Future

Stay ahead with insights into emerging trends and upcoming Smartsheet features, ensuring you're ready to adapt to evolving project management demands.

Who Is This Book For?

This book is ideal for project managers, team leaders, business owners, and professionals across industries looking to improve their project outcomes with Smartsheet. Whether you're just starting out or are a seasoned user, the strategies and insights provided here will help you elevate your approach to project management.

Let's Get Started!

By the end of this book, you'll have a solid understanding of Smartsheet's capabilities and how to apply them to achieve project success. So, let's dive in and begin your journey to mastering Smartsheet!

Section 1:
Getting Started with Smartsheet

Introduction to Smartsheet and Its Core Concepts

Welcome to the first chapter of **"Smartsheet Strategies: Driving Project Success."** Smartsheet is a dynamic, cloud-based platform that revolutionizes the way organizations and teams manage projects, collaborate, and achieve goals. In this chapter, we'll introduce you to Smartsheet, its purpose, and the fundamental concepts that will serve as the foundation for your journey.

What is Smartsheet?

Smartsheet is a work management and collaboration platform that combines the functionality of spreadsheets with the power of project management tools. It's designed to help teams streamline workflows, enhance communication, and improve overall productivity. Smartsheet is widely used across industries, from small businesses to Fortune 500 companies, because of its versatility and scalability.

Key Features of Smartsheet:

- **Spreadsheet-Like Interface**: Familiar layout that simplifies adoption and reduces the learning curve.
- **Real-Time Collaboration**: Enables team members to work together simultaneously, regardless of location.
- **Automation**: Automates repetitive tasks to save time and reduce errors.
- **Customizable Dashboards**: Provides insights and metrics for better decision-making.
- **Integration**: Connects with popular tools like Microsoft Teams, Slack, and Google Workspace.

The Core Concepts of Smartsheet

Understanding the foundational elements of Smartsheet will help you use it effectively. These core concepts define how data is structured, organized, and utilized within the platform.

1. Sheets

A **sheet** is the central workspace in Smartsheet, where all your data resides. It's similar to a spreadsheet but offers enhanced functionality tailored for project management. Sheets are highly customizable and can accommodate a wide range of use cases, including task tracking, resource allocation, and budget management.

Key elements of a sheet include:

- **Rows and Columns**: Organize your data in a structured format.
- **Cells**: Hold various types of information, such as text, dates, and dropdown lists.
- **Attachments and Comments**: Allow additional context and collaboration within rows.

2. Reports

Reports enable you to pull data from multiple sheets and present it in a consolidated view. This is particularly useful for tracking progress across projects or creating summaries for stakeholders.

3. Dashboards

Dashboards are visual, interactive displays that provide real-time insights into your projects. They can include charts, graphs, and widgets to highlight key metrics and trends.

4. Templates

Smartsheet offers a library of pre-built templates to help you get started quickly. Templates are designed for common use cases, such as project planning, marketing campaigns, and event management.

5. Workspaces

A workspace is a shared area where you can organize related sheets, reports, and dashboards. It's ideal for managing large projects or departmental initiatives, ensuring all resources are accessible in one location.

How Smartsheet Drives Success

Smartsheet isn't just a tool—it's a comprehensive solution for managing complex projects and achieving results. Here's how Smartsheet can drive success for your team:

1. **Enhanced Collaboration**: Break down silos by enabling team members to work together in real-time.
2. **Increased Productivity**: Automate repetitive tasks and focus on high-value activities.
3. **Improved Decision-Making**: Leverage data-driven insights from reports and dashboards.
4. **Scalability**: Adapt Smartsheet to fit the needs of any project, team, or organization.
5. **Flexibility**: Customize sheets, workflows, and automations to align with your processes.

How This Chapter Fits into the Bigger Picture

This chapter lays the groundwork for understanding Smartsheet's potential. In the following chapters of **"Getting Started with Smartsheet,"** you'll learn how to set up your account, navigate the interface, and get comfortable with basic terminology and features. Each concept will build upon the knowledge gained here, empowering you to use Smartsheet with confidence.

Let's move forward and start turning your projects into success stories!

Setting Up Your Smartsheet Account

Before diving into the powerful features of Smartsheet, you need to set up your account. This chapter will guide you step-by-step through the process, ensuring you're ready to start your journey toward smarter project management and collaboration.

Why Set Up Your Smartsheet Account?

Setting up a Smartsheet account is the first step toward unlocking its potential. Whether you're an individual user, a team leader, or part of a large organization, having a well-configured account lays the foundation for efficient planning, tracking, and reporting.

Step 1: Choose the Right Plan

Smartsheet offers various plans tailored to different needs. Selecting the right one depends on your requirements and goals.

Available Plans:

1. **Individual Plan**:
   - Ideal for freelancers or solo entrepreneurs.
   - Offers basic features such as sheet creation and collaboration.
2. **Business Plan**:
   - Suited for small to medium-sized teams.
   - Includes features like dashboards, reports, and integrations.
3. **Enterprise Plan**:
   - Designed for large organizations with complex needs.
   - Provides advanced security, controls, and premium support.

Pro Tip:

Start with a free trial if you're unsure which plan suits you. Smartsheet allows you to test the platform for a limited time without commitment.

Step 2: Create Your Account

1. **Visit Smartsheet's Website**
   Go to [www.smartsheet.com] (http://www.smartsheet.com) and click on the "Sign Up" or "Try Smartsheet for Free" button.
2. **Enter Your Information**
   - Provide your **name** and **email address**.
   - Create a **strong password**.
3. **Choose a Plan**
   - Select the plan that aligns with your needs.
   - If starting with a free trial, no payment information is required initially.
4. **Verify Your Email**
   - Check your inbox for a verification email from Smartsheet.
   - Click the link to activate your account.

Step 3: Configure Your Profile

After logging into your account for the first time, take a few minutes to set up your profile:

1. **Add a Profile Picture**: Personalize your account for easier identification in collaborative projects.
2. **Set Your Time Zone**: Ensure deadlines and schedules are accurate based on your location.
3. **Customize Notification Settings**: Decide how and when you'd like to receive updates about project activities.

Step 4: Explore Your Workspace

Once your account is set up, familiarize yourself with the default workspace provided by Smartsheet:

1. **Home Screen**:
   - This is your central hub for accessing sheets, reports, and dashboards.
   - Use the search bar to quickly find what you need.
2. **Sheets Section**:
   - Create and manage sheets for your projects.
   - Explore pre-built templates available for various use cases.
3. **Apps and Integrations**:
   - Check out Smartsheet's app marketplace to explore integrations with other tools you use.

Step 5: Set Up Your First Sheet

To start working right away, create your first sheet:

1. **Click the + (Create) Button**: Found on the left sidebar or home screen.
2. **Choose an Option**:
   - Build a sheet from scratch.
   - Use a template for a specific project type.
3. **Save Your Sheet**: Give it a clear, descriptive name to ensure it's easy to find later.

Step 6: Invite Team Members

Collaboration is at the heart of Smartsheet. If you're working with a team:

1. **Invite Members**:
   - Go to the "Share" button in the top-right corner of your sheet.
   - Enter the email addresses of your team members.
2. **Set Permissions**:
   - **Viewer**: Can only view the sheet.
   - **Editor**: Can edit the sheet's content.
   - **Admin**: Has full control over the sheet.

Troubleshooting Common Setup Issues

1. **Didn't Receive the Verification Email?**
   - Check your spam or junk folder.
   - Ensure you entered the correct email address during sign-up.

2. **Can't Log In?**
   - Double-check your email and password.
   - Use the "Forgot Password" option if needed.
3. **Billing Questions?**
   - Visit the billing section in your account settings for details about your subscription.

Wrapping Up

Congratulations! You've successfully set up your Smartsheet account. With your profile configured and your first sheet ready to go, you're now prepared to explore Smartsheet's features in detail.

Navigating the Smartsheet Interface

To leverage the full potential of Smartsheet, it's essential to understand its interface. In this chapter, we'll take you on a detailed tour of Smartsheet's layout, features, and tools, ensuring that you feel comfortable navigating the platform and accessing its powerful capabilities.

Overview of the Smartsheet Interface

The Smartsheet interface is designed to be intuitive and user-friendly, providing you with the tools to manage projects and collaborate seamlessly. Here's what you'll encounter when you log in:

Main Components

1. **Home Screen**
   - Your starting point for accessing recent sheets, reports, and dashboards.
   - Displays your most frequently used items for quick access.
2. **Navigation Bar (Left Sidebar)**
   - A persistent menu on the left side of the screen.
   - Provides access to key sections like:
     - **Home**: View your workspace and recent items.
     - **Sheets**: Create or access existing sheets.
     - **Reports**: Manage custom reports for your projects.
     - **Dashboards**: View and build interactive project dashboards.
3. **Toolbar (Top of the Screen)**
   - Offers context-specific tools based on the sheet, report, or dashboard you're viewing.
   - Includes buttons for adding rows, sharing, creating automations, and more.
4. **Sheet View**
   - The central workspace where you can view and edit your sheets.
   - Contains rows and columns similar to a spreadsheet, with added functionality like attachments, comments, and conditional formatting.

Key Sections of the Interface

1. The Home Tab

The **Home Tab** serves as your launchpad, providing an overview of your most important items. Features include:

- **Favorites**: Pin frequently used sheets or dashboards for quick access.
- **Recents**: See your recently accessed items.
- **Workspaces**: Organize your sheets, reports, and dashboards into shared folders for easy collaboration.

2. Sheets Section

The **Sheets Section** is where you create and manage your project sheets.

- **Create a New Sheet**: Use the "+" icon to start from scratch or select a template.
- **Search Bar**: Quickly locate a specific sheet by typing its name.
- **Sheet Types**:

- ○ Grid View
- ○ Card View
- ○ Gantt Chart View
- ○ Calendar View

---

3. Reports Section

Reports are used to consolidate and filter data across multiple sheets.

- **Create Reports**: Use the "Create" button to build reports tailored to your project needs.
- **Filter Options**: Set conditions to display only the data relevant to you.
- **Interactive Elements**: Reports update automatically as sheet data changes, ensuring real-time accuracy.

---

4. Dashboards Section

Dashboards are interactive and visual tools for tracking project performance.

- **Widgets**: Add charts, graphs, metrics, or text elements.
- **Customizable Layouts**: Arrange widgets to display the most critical information for your team.
- **Sharing Options**: Easily share dashboards with stakeholders for transparent reporting.

---

5. Account Menu

Located in the top-right corner, the account menu allows you to:

- **Update Profile Settings**
- **Adjust Notification Preferences**
- **Switch Between Accounts** (if you manage multiple accounts).

Views in Smartsheet

Smartsheet offers several views to accommodate different project management needs. You can switch between these views using the toolbar:

1. **Grid View**:
   - ○ Default view, similar to a spreadsheet.
   - ○ Ideal for data entry and general management.
2. **Card View**:
   - ○ Presents rows as cards, perfect for Kanban-style task management.
   - ○ Drag and drop cards to change statuses or categories.
3. **Gantt Chart View**:
   - ○ Visualizes timelines and dependencies.
   - ○ Useful for planning schedules and tracking milestones.
4. **Calendar View**:
   - ○ Displays rows with date fields in a calendar format.
   - ○ Great for scheduling and visualizing deadlines.

Navigating Within a Sheet

Once you open a sheet, you'll find several important features:

1. **Column Headers**: Define the type of data stored in each column (e.g., text, dropdown, date).
2. **Row Numbers**: Help you reference and organize data easily.
3. **Attachments and Comments**: Add context to specific rows by attaching files or leaving comments.
4. **Conditional Formatting**: Highlight rows or cells based on specific criteria to draw attention to key information.
5. **Filters**: Show or hide rows based on conditions to focus on relevant data.

Pro Tips for Efficient Navigation

1. **Keyboard Shortcuts**
   - Use shortcuts to save time. For example, press "Ctrl + /" (Windows) or "Cmd + /" (Mac) to view the complete list of shortcuts.
2. **Search Functionality**
   - The global search bar allows you to locate sheets, reports, or dashboards across your account instantly.
3. **Pinned Items**
   - Pin your most-used sheets and dashboards to the sidebar for one-click access.
4. **Customization**
   - Rearrange columns or adjust row heights to create a layout that works best for you.

Wrapping Up

Mastering the Smartsheet interface is a crucial step toward maximizing your productivity. By understanding how to navigate the platform, locate key features, and utilize different views, you're now equipped to handle projects with confidence.

Basic Terminology and Key Features

Understanding the terminology and features of Smartsheet is crucial for navigating the platform effectively and leveraging its full capabilities. This chapter will define essential terms and introduce key features that form the backbone of Smartsheet's functionality.

Basic Terminology

Before diving deeper into Smartsheet, it's important to familiarize yourself with the following terms:

1. Sheets

A **sheet** is the primary workspace in Smartsheet where data is entered and managed. Sheets can be customized to fit your project's specific needs and are used for planning, tracking, and reporting.

2. Rows and Columns

- **Rows**: Horizontal sections in a sheet where you input specific items, tasks, or data points.
- **Columns**: Vertical sections in a sheet, each with a predefined type (e.g., text, date, dropdown). Columns organize your data and provide structure.

3. Cells

A **cell** is the intersection of a row and a column. Each cell can contain various types of data, including text, numbers, dates, or links to other resources.

4. Attachments and Comments

- **Attachments**: Files, images, or links that can be added to specific rows for additional context.
- **Comments**: Notes or discussions associated with rows, enabling team collaboration directly within the sheet.

5. Workspaces

A **workspace** is a shared area for organizing related sheets, reports, and dashboards. Workspaces are particularly useful for managing multiple projects or collaborating within a team.

6. Reports

Reports pull data from one or more sheets to create a consolidated view. They are dynamic and update automatically as changes are made to the source sheets.

7. Dashboards

Dashboards are visual representations of key project metrics and insights. They use widgets, such as charts and graphs, to provide a real-time overview of progress and performance.

8. Filters

Filters allow you to display only the data that meets specific criteria. They are essential for focusing on the most relevant information in a large sheet.

9. Automation Rules

Automation rules enable you to automate repetitive tasks, such as sending notifications, updating statuses, or creating alerts based on predefined triggers and conditions.

10. Formulas

Formulas in Smartsheet function similarly to those in traditional spreadsheets, allowing you to perform calculations, manipulate data, and link information across sheets.

Key Features

Now that we've covered the terminology, let's explore some of Smartsheet's key features that make it a powerful tool for project management.

1. Grid View

The default view in Smartsheet, **Grid View** resembles a traditional spreadsheet but with added capabilities for collaboration and automation.

2. Gantt Chart View

The **Gantt Chart View** provides a timeline visualization of your project, showing task dependencies, milestones, and durations. This view is especially useful for scheduling and resource planning.

3. Card View

Card View displays rows as movable cards, perfect for managing tasks in a Kanban-style workflow. You can drag and drop cards between columns to update statuses or categories.

4. Calendar View

The **Calendar View** shows tasks and deadlines in a calendar format, making it easier to track events and schedule activities.

5. Conditional Formatting

This feature allows you to automatically apply formatting (e.g., color changes) to cells or rows based on specific conditions. Conditional formatting helps highlight important information or flag potential issues.

6. Cell Linking

Cell linking enables you to connect data between sheets, ensuring that changes made in one location are reflected in another. This feature is ideal for creating dashboards and reports that rely on multiple data sources.

7. Integrations

Smartsheet integrates with a wide range of third-party tools, including Microsoft Teams, Slack, Google Workspace, and Salesforce. These integrations streamline workflows and improve productivity.

8. Forms

Forms allow you to collect data from users and automatically populate it into a Smartsheet. They are useful for surveys, event registrations, or gathering feedback.

9. Automation and Alerts

Smartsheet's automation tools let you set up workflows to trigger specific actions, such as sending reminders or updating statuses. Alerts notify team members about changes or deadlines.

10. Activity Log

The activity log tracks all changes made to a sheet, providing a detailed history of who did what and when. This is essential for maintaining accountability and tracking progress.

Practical Applications of Key Features

Here's how the basic terminology and key features come together in real-world scenarios:

- **Project Management**: Use sheets, Gantt charts, and dashboards to plan, track, and report on project progress.
- **Team Collaboration**: Leverage comments, attachments, and real-time updates to enhance communication and streamline workflows.
- **Data Consolidation**: Create reports and dashboards to aggregate information across multiple sheets for a comprehensive view of performance.
- **Automation**: Set up rules to automate repetitive tasks, freeing up time for strategic activities.

Wrapping Up

Familiarity with Smartsheet's terminology and features is essential for navigating the platform confidently. These foundational elements will be revisited and built upon as you progress through the book.

Section 2:
Creating and Customizing Sheets

Building Your First Sheet from Scratch

Creating a sheet from scratch is one of the most empowering aspects of using Smartsheet. By building a custom sheet, you can tailor it to your specific project requirements and set the foundation for effective planning, tracking, and collaboration. In this chapter, we'll guide you step-by-step through the process of creating your first sheet.

What is a Sheet?

A **sheet** in Smartsheet is more than just a spreadsheet—it's a dynamic workspace designed for project management. It can be used to track tasks, manage resources, monitor budgets, and much more. Building a sheet from scratch gives you complete control over its structure and functionality.

Step 1: Create a New Sheet

1. **Log In to Smartsheet**
   ○ Start by logging in to your Smartsheet account at [www.smartsheet.com] (http://www.smartsheet.com).
2. **Access the Creation Menu**
   ○ On the left navigation bar, click the "+" button (Create) and select **Sheet** from the dropdown menu.
3. **Name Your Sheet**
   ○ Give your sheet a clear and descriptive name that reflects its purpose. For example, "Marketing Campaign Tracker" or "Project Management Overview."

Step 2: Define the Columns

Columns are the backbone of your sheet, defining the type of data you'll track. Smartsheet provides several predefined column types to suit different needs.

1. **Set Up Your Primary Column**
   ○ The first column is the **Primary Column**, which acts as the key identifier for each row. Use it to list tasks, item names, or categories.
2. **Add Additional Columns**
   ○ Click the **+ Add Column** button to create more columns.
   ○ Examples of common columns:
      ■ **Task Name** (Text/Number)
      ■ **Assigned To** (Contact List)
      ■ **Start Date** (Date)
      ■ **End Date** (Date)
      ■ **Status** (Dropdown)

- **Priority** (Dropdown or Symbols)
3. **Customize Column Types**
   - Choose the appropriate type for each column:
     - **Text/Number**: For general information or numeric values.
     - **Dropdown List**: For predefined options like "High," "Medium," "Low."
     - **Date**: To track deadlines or schedule milestones.
     - **Checkbox**: To indicate completed tasks or approvals.
     - **Contact List**: For team members or stakeholders.
4. **Use Column Descriptions**
   - Add descriptions to your columns to clarify their purpose, especially if others will collaborate on the sheet.

Step 3: Populate Your Sheet

Once your columns are set up, start adding rows to populate your sheet:

1. **Enter Data**
   - Add tasks, deadlines, assignments, or any other relevant information row by row.
2. **Utilize Dropdowns and Symbols**
   - Select predefined values from dropdowns to maintain consistency.
   - Use symbols (like flags or stars) for visual indicators of priority or completion.
3. **Add Attachments and Comments**
   - Attach files directly to rows for quick reference.
   - Use comments to provide additional context or facilitate discussions with collaborators.

Step 4: Save and Share Your Sheet

1. **Save Your Work**
   - Smartsheet autosaves your changes, but it's a good habit to confirm by clicking the **Save** icon in the toolbar.
2. **Invite Collaborators**
   - Click the **Share** button in the top-right corner.
   - Enter the email addresses of team members or stakeholders.
   - Assign permissions:
     - **Viewer**: Can only view the sheet.
     - **Editor**: Can make changes to the sheet.
     - **Admin**: Has full control over the sheet.

Step 5: Customize the View

Smartsheet allows you to visualize your data in different ways based on your needs:

1. **Grid View**
   - Ideal for data entry and general management.
2. **Card View**
   - Switch to Card View for Kanban-style task tracking. Drag and drop cards to update statuses or priorities.
3. **Gantt Chart View**
   - Visualize timelines and dependencies for tasks. Enable Gantt view by adding start and end date columns and selecting the Gantt icon.

4. **Calendar View**
   - Use the Calendar View to display tasks or events on a calendar.

Step 6: Add Conditional Formatting

Conditional formatting helps highlight important information or flag potential issues:

1. **Create Rules**
   - Navigate to the toolbar and select **Conditional Formatting**.
   - Define rules based on specific criteria, such as:
     - Highlight overdue tasks in red.
     - Mark high-priority items with bold text or a specific color.
2. **Apply Rules**
   - Assign the rules to relevant rows or columns for automatic formatting.

Step 7: Automate Your Sheet

Automation saves time and ensures consistency in your workflows:

1. **Set Up Alerts and Reminders**
   - Navigate to the **Automation** menu and create rules for notifications. For example:
     - Notify team members when a task is assigned.
     - Send reminders for approaching deadlines.
2. **Define Approval Processes**
   - Automate approvals by setting triggers when a status changes or when a specific condition is met.

Pro Tips for Success

- **Start Simple**: Focus on essential columns and gradually expand as your needs evolve.
- **Use Templates for Inspiration**: Review Smartsheet's library of templates to get ideas for structuring your sheet.
- **Leverage Help Resources**: Smartsheet offers tutorials and guides to assist with customization.

Wrapping Up

By following these steps, you've created your first sheet from scratch in Smartsheet. This custom sheet will serve as a foundation for managing your projects efficiently and effectively.

Working with Pre-Built Templates

Pre-built templates are one of Smartsheet's most powerful features, providing a quick and efficient way to get started on your projects. These templates are designed for a variety of use cases and industries, helping you save time while maintaining a professional structure. In this chapter, we'll explore how to find, use, and customize pre-built templates to meet your project's unique requirements.

Why Use Pre-Built Templates?

Templates offer several benefits, including:

1. **Time Savings**: Skip the setup process and start working immediately.
2. **Consistency**: Maintain a standardized structure across your projects.
3. **Guidance**: Templates often come with built-in features, such as columns, formulas, and conditional formatting, that align with best practices.
4. **Customization**: Every template is fully customizable, allowing you to tailor it to your specific needs.

Accessing Smartsheet's Template Library

To explore and use pre-built templates:

1. **Navigate to the Template Library**
   - Log in to your Smartsheet account.
   - From the Home tab, click **"+ Create"** and select **"Browse Templates"**.
2. **Explore Categories**
   Templates are organized into categories for easy navigation. Common categories include:
   - **Project Management**
   - **Marketing**
   - **Event Planning**
   - **IT and Software Development**
   - **HR and Onboarding**
3. **Preview Templates**
   - Click on a template to view its structure and features.
   - Look for elements such as Gantt charts, task lists, or dashboards that align with your project goals.
4. **Select a Template**
   - Once you've identified a suitable template, click **"Use Template"** to add it to your workspace.

Customizing Pre-Built Templates

While templates provide a solid foundation, customizing them ensures they align perfectly with your project's needs. Here's how to make modifications:

1. Edit Columns and Rows

- **Rename Columns**: Double-click the column header to give it a more relevant name.
- **Add or Remove Columns**: Right-click on a column header to insert or delete columns as needed.
- **Adjust Row Data**: Replace placeholder text with your project's specific information.

2. Modify Views

Templates often come with multiple views, such as Gantt charts or card views. Adjust these views to suit your workflow:

- **Switch Views**: Use the toolbar to toggle between grid, Gantt, card, or calendar views.
- **Update Dependencies**: If the template includes task dependencies, ensure they reflect your project's timeline.

3. Update Formatting and Design

- **Conditional Formatting**: Review and adjust rules to highlight critical information.
- **Colors and Themes**: Apply colors that align with your organization's branding or project priorities.

4. Integrate Automation

Enhance the template's functionality by adding automation rules:

- Set reminders for approaching deadlines.
- Automate status updates based on task completion.

Commonly Used Templates

Here are examples of popular Smartsheet templates and their applications:

1. Project Management Template

- **Purpose**: Plan and track tasks, timelines, and milestones.
- **Features**: Gantt chart, task dependencies, and status tracking.
- **Use Case**: Managing cross-functional team projects.

2. Event Planning Template

- **Purpose**: Coordinate event logistics, schedules, and vendor management.
- **Features**: Task lists, budget trackers, and contact information.
- **Use Case**: Planning conferences, workshops, or corporate events.

3. Marketing Campaign Template

- **Purpose**: Organize campaign goals, deliverables, and performance metrics.
- **Features**: Content calendar, KPI tracking, and task assignments.
- **Use Case**: Launching new products or running digital ad campaigns.

4. IT Project Plan Template

- **Purpose**: Manage technical implementations and software development cycles.
- **Features**: Sprint planning, issue tracking, and backlog management.
- **Use Case**: Developing and deploying software applications.

Best Practices for Using Templates

1. **Start with a Template That Closely Matches Your Needs**
   Even if it's not a perfect fit, starting with a relevant template minimizes the work required to customize it.

2. **Review Pre-Built Formulas and Automation**
   Templates often include formulas and automation rules. Ensure these align with your project's goals and adjust them if necessary.
3. **Collaborate with Your Team**
   Share the template with your team early on. Gather feedback and make adjustments to ensure it meets everyone's needs.
4. **Save Your Custom Template**
   If you've made significant changes to a pre-built template, save it as a new template for future use. This ensures consistency across similar projects.

Wrapping Up

Pre-built templates are a valuable resource for starting your projects efficiently while maintaining a professional structure. By selecting and customizing the right template, you can streamline your workflow and focus on achieving your goals.

Customizing Columns, Rows, and Cell Properties

Customizing columns, rows, and cell properties in Smartsheet is essential for creating a sheet that meets your specific project requirements. By tailoring these elements, you can organize data effectively, enhance visibility, and improve collaboration among team members. This chapter provides a step-by-step guide to customizing your sheets.

Importance of Customization

Customizing columns, rows, and cell properties allows you to:

1. **Improve Clarity**: Organize and present data in a way that's easy to understand.
2. **Enhance Productivity**: Enable team members to find and update information quickly.
3. **Support Automation**: Align columns and cell properties with automation rules for seamless workflows.

Customizing Columns

Columns are the backbone of any sheet, defining the type of data you'll collect and how it's organized.

1. Adding and Removing Columns

- **To Add a Column**:
  - Click the **+ Add Column** button on the right side of the sheet.
  - Select the desired column type and name it appropriately.
- **To Remove a Column**:
  - Right-click the column header and select **Delete Column**.

2. Column Types and Their Uses

- **Text/Number**: For general data like task names or numeric values.
- **Dropdown List**: For predefined options such as task statuses (e.g., "In Progress," "Completed").
- **Date**: For scheduling and deadlines.
- **Checkbox**: To mark completion or approvals.
- **Contact List**: For assigning tasks to specific individuals.
- **Symbols**: For visual indicators like priorities (e.g., stars or flags).

3. Renaming Columns

- Double-click the column header to rename it.
- Use clear, descriptive names to avoid confusion among team members.

4. Reordering Columns

- Drag and drop column headers to reorder them based on priority or workflow requirements.

5. Setting Default Values

- Assign default values to columns to streamline data entry.
  - Example: Set a default status as "Not Started" in a dropdown column.

Customizing Rows

Rows contain the individual data entries in your sheet. Customizing them enhances the organization and usability of your data.

1. Adding and Deleting Rows

- **To Add a Row**:
  - Right-click on a row number and select **Insert Row Above** or **Insert Row Below**.
- **To Delete a Row**:
  - Right-click on the row number and select **Delete Row**.

2. Reordering Rows

- Drag and drop rows to change their order. This is especially useful for reprioritizing tasks or organizing categories.

3. Indenting and Outdenting Rows

- **Indent Rows**: Create subtasks or hierarchical structures by indenting rows.
  - Right-click a row and select **Indent Row**.
- **Outdent Rows**: Remove indentation to promote subtasks back to the main task level.

4. Adding Attachments and Comments

- Attach files to rows by clicking the **Paperclip Icon** in the row menu.
- Add comments to rows for additional context by selecting the **Comment Icon**.

Customizing Cell Properties

Cells are the intersection of rows and columns, where data is entered. Customizing their properties ensures data consistency and enhances visual cues.

1. Data Validation

- Restrict data input to specific types (e.g., numbers only) or predefined options (via dropdown lists).
- Ensure accurate and consistent data across your sheet.

2. Cell Formatting

- **Text Formatting**: Bold, italicize, or underline text for emphasis.
- **Color Formatting**: Apply background or text colors to highlight important data.
  - Example: Use green for completed tasks and red for overdue tasks.

3. Conditional Formatting

- Set rules to automatically format cells based on specific conditions.
  - Example: Highlight tasks with a "High" priority in bold red text.
- Access conditional formatting from the toolbar and define rules based on column data.

4. Cell Linking

- Link cells between sheets to maintain consistency and avoid duplication of data.
  - Right-click a cell and select **Link from Cell in Another Sheet**.

5. Freezing Columns and Rows

- Freeze specific rows or columns to keep them visible while scrolling through the sheet.
  - Access the freeze options from the **View Menu**.

Practical Applications of Customization

Example 1: Task Management

- Use a **Checkbox Column** to track completed tasks.
- Add a **Dropdown Column** for status updates (e.g., "In Progress," "Completed").
- Apply **Conditional Formatting** to highlight overdue tasks in red.

Example 2: Resource Allocation

- Create a **Contact List Column** to assign tasks to team members.
- Add a **Text/Number Column** for estimated hours or costs.
- Use **Cell Linking** to connect resource data across multiple sheets.

Example 3: Project Reporting

- Use **Symbols Columns** to indicate task priorities visually.
- Apply **Freeze Panes** to keep column headers visible during report reviews.

Pro Tips for Customization

1. **Keep It Simple**: Start with essential columns and rows, and expand as your project grows.
2. **Use Descriptive Labels**: Ensure column and row names clearly describe their purpose.
3. **Test Conditional Formatting**: Apply formatting rules incrementally to avoid overwhelming your sheet.
4. **Regularly Review Structure**: Periodically check your sheet to ensure it aligns with your project goals.

Wrapping Up

Customizing columns, rows, and cell properties is a powerful way to tailor Smartsheet to your specific needs. By implementing these techniques, you can create a sheet that is both functional and visually appealing, ensuring better project management and collaboration.

Sorting, Filtering, and Grouping Data

Organizing data effectively is a key component of successful project management. Smartsheet offers powerful tools for sorting, filtering, and grouping data, enabling you to analyze information, identify patterns, and prioritize tasks efficiently. In this chapter, we'll explore how to leverage these tools to maximize your productivity.

The Importance of Data Organization

Data organization helps you:

1. **Streamline Workflows**: Quickly locate and update critical information.
2. **Enhance Clarity**: Make large datasets easier to understand and manage.
3. **Improve Decision-Making**: Focus on relevant data to make informed decisions.

Sorting Data

Sorting data rearranges rows based on the values in specific columns. This is particularly useful for prioritizing tasks or organizing entries alphabetically.

1. Sorting by a Single Column

- Right-click the column header and select **Sort Rows**.
- Choose **Ascending** or **Descending** order.
  - Example: Sort tasks by priority (e.g., High to Low).

2. Sorting by Multiple Columns

- Open the **Sort Rows** dialog by selecting it from the toolbar.
- Add sorting criteria for multiple columns.
  - Example: First, sort by **Status** (e.g., Completed, In Progress), then by **Due Date**.
- Click **Apply** to execute the sort.

Best Practices for Sorting:

- Always save your sheet before sorting to preserve the original order.
- Avoid sorting by a column with merged cells, as this can cause errors.

Filtering Data

Filters allow you to display only the rows that meet specific criteria, making it easier to focus on the most relevant data.

1. Applying Filters

- Click the **Filter** icon in the toolbar.
- Define filter criteria based on column values.
  - Example: Show only tasks with a status of "In Progress."

2. Custom Filters

- Create custom filters by combining multiple conditions.
  - Example: Display tasks assigned to a specific team member that are due within the next week.
- Use operators such as **equals**, **contains**, or **is blank** to refine results.

3. Saving Filters

- Save frequently used filters for quick access.
- To save a filter, click **Save as New Filter** after setting your criteria.

Best Practices for Filtering:

- Communicate with collaborators before applying filters, as they affect everyone viewing the sheet.
- Use filters to focus on specific aspects of your project during meetings or reviews.

Grouping Data

Grouping data involves categorizing rows based on shared attributes, allowing you to view your information in a structured hierarchy.

1. Using Indentation for Grouping

- Indent rows to create subtasks or group related items under a parent task.
  - Example: Group all tasks for a specific milestone under its header row.
- Right-click a row and select **Indent Row** to nest it under the row above.

2. Creating Categories with Symbols or Dropdowns

- Add a **Dropdown Column** with predefined categories.
  - Example: Categorize tasks by department (e.g., Marketing, IT, HR).
- Use **Card View** to group tasks visually by their dropdown category.

3. Leveraging Conditional Formatting for Grouping

- Apply conditional formatting rules to highlight grouped data.
  - Example: Assign unique colors to tasks based on their assigned team.

Combining Sorting, Filtering, and Grouping

Using these features together creates a dynamic and organized workspace:

1. **Sort** tasks by due date to prioritize deadlines.
2. **Filter** to display only tasks assigned to a specific team member.
3. **Group** tasks by project phase using dropdown categories.

This combination provides a clear, actionable view of your project data.

Practical Applications

Example 1: Task Prioritization

- Sort tasks by priority (High, Medium, Low).
- Filter to show only tasks due within the next week.

Example 2: Resource Allocation

- Group tasks by department or team member.
- Filter to display tasks with overdue deadlines for targeted follow-ups.

Example 3: Progress Tracking

- Sort by status (Not Started, In Progress, Completed).
- Apply conditional formatting to highlight overdue tasks.

Pro Tips for Data Organization

1. **Use Default Views**: Save sorted, filtered, or grouped views for regular use.
2. **Communicate Changes**: Notify collaborators when applying filters or sorting to avoid confusion.
3. **Leverage Automation**: Combine sorting and filtering with automation rules to update data dynamically.

Wrapping Up

Sorting, filtering, and grouping data are essential skills for managing projects in Smartsheet. By mastering these tools, you can keep your sheets organized, focus on key information, and enhance team productivity.

Section 3:
Collaboration and Sharing

Inviting Team Members and Setting Permissions

Collaboration is a cornerstone of successful project management, and Smartsheet excels at enabling teamwork. By inviting team members to your sheets and assigning appropriate permissions, you can ensure that everyone stays informed and engaged while maintaining control over your project data. This chapter provides a comprehensive guide to inviting collaborators and setting permissions effectively.

Why Collaboration Matters

Bringing team members into Smartsheet offers several advantages:

1. **Real-Time Updates**: Keep everyone on the same page with live changes.
2. **Centralized Communication**: Share files, comments, and updates directly within the platform.
3. **Controlled Access**: Assign roles and permissions to safeguard sensitive data.

Inviting Team Members

1. Sharing Your Sheet

To invite team members to a sheet:

1. Open the sheet you want to share.
2. Click the **Share** button in the top-right corner.
3. Enter the email addresses of the people you want to invite.
4. Add an optional message to provide context for your invitation.
5. Click **Send**.

2. Sharing Workspaces

If you're managing multiple related sheets, consider sharing the entire workspace:

1. Open the desired workspace.
2. Click the **Share** button in the workspace menu.
3. Enter the email addresses of collaborators.
4. Assign permissions for the workspace as a whole (explained below).

Understanding Permissions

Smartsheet offers a range of permission levels to ensure that users can only access and modify data as appropriate.

1. Viewer

- **Access**: View-only access to the sheet.

- **Ideal For**: Stakeholders who need to monitor progress but don't need to make changes.

2. Editor

- **Access**: Edit rows, add attachments, and comment.
- **Ideal For**: Team members actively working on tasks.

3. Admin

- **Access**: Full control over the sheet, including sharing and modifying structure.
- **Ideal For**: Project managers or team leads.

4. Owner

- **Access**: The highest level of control, reserved for the sheet creator or transferred by the owner.
- **Unique Capability**: Only the owner can delete the sheet.

Setting Permissions

1. Assigning Permissions While Sharing

- During the sharing process, use the dropdown menu next to each email address to select the appropriate permission level.
- Ensure permissions align with the collaborator's role and responsibilities.

2. Adjusting Permissions Later

- Open the **Share** menu for the sheet or workspace.
- Locate the user whose permissions you want to change.
- Select a new permission level from the dropdown menu.

3. Removing Access

- To revoke a user's access, open the **Share** menu and click the **X** next to their name.

Sharing Best Practices

1. Define Roles Clearly

- Before sharing, outline each team member's role and responsibilities.
- Assign permissions based on these roles to avoid confusion.

2. Limit Admin Access

- Restrict admin permissions to key personnel to prevent unauthorized changes.

3. Communicate Expectations

- Use the optional message feature when sharing to explain what collaborators should focus on.

4. Regularly Review Permissions

- Periodically audit your shared sheets and workspaces to ensure permissions remain appropriate.

Advanced Sharing Options

1. Public Sharing

- Smartsheet allows you to share sheets publicly via a link.
- Use this feature cautiously and only for non-sensitive data.

2. Domain-Restricted Sharing

- For enterprise accounts, restrict sharing to users within your organization's domain for enhanced security.

3. Requesting Access

- Users without permissions can request access to a sheet. Owners and admins will receive a notification to approve or deny the request.

Troubleshooting Sharing Issues

1. Collaborator Didn't Receive the Invite

- Ask them to check their spam folder.
- Resend the invitation if necessary.

2. Can't Edit the Sheet

- Verify that their permission level is set to **Editor** or higher.

3. Too Many Users

- Smartsheet's user limit for shared sheets depends on your subscription plan. Consider upgrading if needed.

Real-World Applications

Example 1: Project Planning

- Invite team members as **Editors** to update task statuses and deadlines.
- Add stakeholders as **Viewers** to monitor progress without making changes.

Example 2: Event Management

- Assign admins to manage logistics and update schedules.
- Share a public link to the event schedule with attendees.

Example 3: Budget Tracking

- Limit access to sensitive financial data by assigning **Viewer** permissions to most users while keeping a small team of **Editors** responsible for updates.

Wrapping Up: Inviting team members and setting permissions in Smartsheet ensures that collaboration is efficient, secure, and well-organized. By mastering these processes, you'll create a seamless environment where everyone can contribute to project success.

Real-Time Collaboration Techniques

Real-time collaboration is one of Smartsheet's most powerful features, enabling teams to work together seamlessly on projects, regardless of location. In this chapter, we'll explore practical techniques for maximizing collaboration using Smartsheet, ensuring that your team stays connected, informed, and productive.

The Importance of Real-Time Collaboration

Effective collaboration leads to:

1. **Improved Communication**: Team members can instantly share updates and feedback.
2. **Enhanced Productivity**: Reduce delays caused by outdated information.
3. **Streamlined Workflows**: Centralize tasks, discussions, and files in a single platform.

Real-Time Collaboration Features in Smartsheet

Smartsheet offers several features that facilitate real-time collaboration:

1. Simultaneous Editing

- Multiple users can edit a sheet simultaneously without overwriting changes.
- All updates are visible in real time, ensuring that everyone works from the latest information.
- Changes are automatically saved, reducing the risk of data loss.

2. Activity Log

- The activity log provides a history of all changes made to the sheet.
- Use it to track who made updates and when, ensuring accountability.
- Access the activity log by selecting **File > Activity Log** from the toolbar.

3. Cell Comments

- Add comments to specific cells to provide context or ask questions.
- To add a comment, right-click a cell and select **Add Comment**.
- Comments are tagged with the author's name and timestamp, making it easy to track discussions.

4. File Attachments

- Attach files directly to rows or the entire sheet.
- Use attachments for documents, images, or links relevant to the project.
- Click the **Paperclip Icon** on a row to upload files.

5. Alerts and Notifications

- Set up alerts to notify team members of changes or approaching deadlines.
- Customize notifications to trigger based on specific criteria, such as task status updates or new comments.
- Access these settings through the **Automation** menu.

Techniques for Effective Real-Time Collaboration

1. Use Comments for Context

- Instead of sending emails, leave comments directly on cells or rows.
- Tag team members in comments using **@mention** to notify them.
  - Example: "Please review this task, @JohnDoe."

2. Assign Tasks Clearly

- Use a **Contact List Column** to assign tasks to team members.
- This ensures that everyone knows their responsibilities and deadlines.

3. Implement Conditional Formatting

- Apply conditional formatting to highlight updates or changes.
  - Example: Use bold text or a red background for overdue tasks.

4. Centralize Discussions

- Encourage your team to use Smartsheet's comments and discussions features instead of external communication tools.
- This keeps all project-related conversations in one place for easy reference.

Collaboration in Different Views

1. Grid View

- Ideal for data entry and centralized communication.
- Use this view to focus on specific tasks or details.

2. Card View

- Organize tasks visually using cards in a Kanban-style layout.
- Drag and drop cards to update statuses or priorities.

3. Gantt Chart View

- Collaborate on timelines by adjusting task dependencies and durations.
- Useful for scheduling discussions and aligning project milestones.

4. Calendar View

- Collaborate on event planning by visualizing deadlines and schedules in a calendar format.

Integrating Collaboration with Automation

Enhance real-time collaboration by incorporating automation rules:

1. **Set Up Alerts**
   - Notify team members immediately when tasks are assigned to them.
2. **Automate Status Updates**
   - Use triggers to automatically change task statuses when conditions are met.
3. **Create Reminder Workflows**
   - Send reminders for upcoming deadlines or incomplete tasks.

Best Practices for Real-Time Collaboration

1. **Define Collaboration Norms**
   - Establish clear guidelines for how your team will use Smartsheet for communication and updates.
2. **Encourage Regular Check-Ins**
   - Schedule periodic reviews to discuss updates and address questions directly in Smartsheet.
3. **Monitor Activity Logs**
   - Use activity logs to review recent changes and ensure all updates align with project goals.
4. **Minimize Overlap**
   - Clearly assign tasks to avoid duplication of effort or conflicting updates.
5. **Provide Training**
   - Train team members on Smartsheet's collaboration features to maximize efficiency.

Real-World Applications

Example 1: Marketing Campaign Management

- Collaborate on campaign planning using comments to discuss ideas and approvals.
- Assign tasks to team members with deadlines and notify them of updates in real time.

Example 2: IT Project Coordination

- Use the activity log to track code reviews and changes.
- Attach documentation directly to rows for easy reference during discussions.

Example 3: Event Planning

- Collaborate on schedules using calendar view.
- Use conditional formatting to highlight tasks that require immediate attention.

Wrapping Up

Real-time collaboration techniques are essential for maximizing Smartsheet's potential as a project management tool. By using these features effectively, your team can communicate, update, and execute tasks more efficiently, ensuring project success.

Managing Comments and Discussions

Effective communication is essential for successful project management, and Smartsheet's built-in comments and discussions features are designed to streamline team collaboration. By using these tools, teams can centralize conversations, reduce reliance on external communication platforms, and ensure all relevant information is accessible within the project sheet. This chapter covers the key techniques for managing comments and discussions in Smartsheet.

Why Use Comments and Discussions?

Managing comments and discussions directly in Smartsheet provides several benefits:

1. **Centralized Communication**: Keep all project-related conversations in one place.
2. **Improved Clarity**: Reduce miscommunication by linking comments to specific tasks or data points.
3. **Increased Accountability**: Track who made changes or provided input, with timestamps for each comment.

Adding and Managing Comments

1. Adding a Comment

To add a comment to a row or cell:

1. Right-click the row or cell where you want to add a comment.
2. Select **Add Comment** from the context menu.
3. Type your comment in the text box.
4. Use **@mention** to tag team members (e.g., "@JohnDoe, please review this task").
5. Click **Post** to save the comment.

2. Viewing Comments

- Click the **Comment Icon** in the row to view all associated comments.
- All comments are displayed chronologically, with the author's name and timestamp.

3. Editing and Deleting Comments

- Hover over a comment to reveal the **Edit** or **Delete** option.
- Only the comment author or an admin can edit or delete a comment.

Best Practices for Using Comments

1. **Be Clear and Specific**
   - Provide actionable feedback and include necessary details.
   - Example: Instead of "Fix this," write "Update the delivery date to match the revised schedule."
2. **Tag Relevant Team Members**
   - Use @mentions to notify specific individuals about your comment.
3. **Follow Up on Comments**
   - Resolve issues or complete tasks mentioned in comments promptly.
   - Use comments to confirm completion or provide updates.

4. **Keep Comments Organized**
   - Avoid excessive back-and-forth in a single comment thread. Break discussions into separate comments if needed.

Managing Discussions Across the Sheet

1. Discussion Panel

- Use the **Discussion Panel** to view all comments in a sheet.
- Access the panel by clicking the **Comment Icon** in the toolbar.
- Filter discussions by date, user, or specific rows.

2. Sorting and Searching Comments

- Use the search bar in the discussion panel to locate specific comments.
- Sort comments by recent activity or relevance to streamline navigation.

3. Resolving Conversations

- Mark comments as resolved once the issue has been addressed.
- This helps keep the discussion panel organized and focused on unresolved items.

Attaching Files to Comments

1. Uploading Attachments

- Add relevant files directly to rows or comments to provide additional context.
- Click the **Paperclip Icon** in the row or comment panel to upload files.

2. File Types Supported

- Attach documents, images, spreadsheets, and links to external resources.
- Ensure file names are descriptive for easy identification.

3. Using Attachments for Collaboration

- Share draft versions of documents for review.
- Include reference materials directly within the sheet to eliminate the need for external platforms.

Notifications and Alerts

Smartsheet's notification system ensures that team members stay informed about discussions:

1. **Notification Settings**
   - Customize notification preferences in your account settings.
   - Choose to receive alerts for @mentions, new comments, or all activity in a sheet.
2. **Automation for Discussions**
   - Use automation rules to trigger notifications based on comments.
   - Example: Notify a project manager when a comment includes the word "urgent."
3. **Daily Summary Emails**
   - Enable daily summary emails to receive an overview of all comments and discussions from the previous day.

Troubleshooting Common Issues

1. Missed Notifications

- Ensure team members check their notification settings and email spam folder.
- Encourage collaborators to log in to Smartsheet regularly to stay updated.

2. Overlapping Conversations

- Use @mentions to clarify which team member a comment is directed toward.
- Split large discussions into smaller, focused threads.

3. Misplaced Comments

- Move misplaced comments to the correct row or sheet by copying the text and reposting it in the appropriate location.

Real-World Applications

Example 1: Task Reviews

- Use comments to request reviews of completed tasks.
- Attach relevant files or screenshots for additional context.

Example 2: Change Management

- Centralize discussions about changes to project scope or timelines within the sheet.
- Tag stakeholders for approvals or feedback.

Example 3: Event Planning

- Discuss logistics such as vendor selection or schedule adjustments in row-specific comments.
- Attach contracts, itineraries, or vendor quotes for reference.

Wrapping Up

Managing comments and discussions in Smartsheet keeps your team aligned and informed. By using these tools effectively, you can foster clear communication, enhance accountability, and streamline project collaboration.

Best Practices for Sharing and Version Control

Sharing and version control are vital components of effective collaboration in Smartsheet. Proper sharing practices ensure that your project data is accessible to the right people, while robust version control helps maintain data accuracy and consistency. This chapter will guide you through best practices to maximize security, collaboration, and efficiency.

Why Sharing and Version Control Matter

- **Collaboration**: Sharing allows team members and stakeholders to access and contribute to your project.
- **Accountability**: Version control ensures you can track changes and maintain a reliable project history.
- **Security**: Effective sharing practices protect sensitive data while enabling collaboration.

Best Practices for Sharing

1. Share with the Right People

- **Define Roles**: Identify who needs access to your sheet and why.
- **Assign Appropriate Permissions**: Use Smartsheet's permission levels (Viewer, Editor, Admin) to control access.
    - Example: Grant Viewer access to stakeholders who only need to monitor progress.

2. Use Workspaces for Team Projects

- **Centralize Resources**: Create a workspace for related sheets, reports, and dashboards.
- **Share at the Workspace Level**: This ensures team members have consistent access to all relevant files.

3. Leverage Contact Groups

- **Organize Team Members**: Create contact groups for departments or project teams.
- **Simplify Sharing**: Share sheets with groups instead of individual users to save time.

4. Restrict Public Sharing

- Avoid sharing sensitive data via public links unless necessary.
- Use domain-restricted sharing to limit access to users within your organization.

5. Communicate Expectations

- Notify collaborators of their responsibilities and how they should interact with the sheet.
    - Example: Specify that editors should only update rows assigned to them.

Best Practices for Version Control

1. Save Changes Regularly

- Smartsheet automatically saves changes, but it's a good practice to double-check critical updates.

2. Enable the Activity Log

- The **Activity Log** tracks all changes made to a sheet, including who made them and when.
- Use this feature to monitor updates and resolve discrepancies.

3. Lock Critical Columns or Rows

- Prevent accidental changes to key data by locking columns or rows.
- Only admins and the owner can unlock these elements.

4. Use Backup Copies

- Create periodic backups of your sheets to safeguard against data loss.
  - **To Back Up a Sheet**: Export it as an Excel file or PDF for offline storage.

5. Limit Access to Admins

- Restrict admin permissions to trusted team members to minimize accidental or unauthorized changes.

6. Resolve Conflicts Promptly

- Use the **Discussion Panel** to address conflicting updates.
- Collaborate with team members to clarify and correct changes.

Advanced Sharing and Version Control Features

1. Conditional Formatting for Version Control

- Highlight recent changes or updates using conditional formatting rules.
  - Example: Apply a color to rows updated in the last 24 hours.

2. Automation Rules for Alerts

- Set up notifications for critical updates or changes to specific rows or columns.
- Example: Notify the owner when a task's status changes to "Complete."

3. Access Reports for Sharing

- Use reports to consolidate data from multiple sheets and share only relevant information.
  - Example: Share a filtered report showing progress on top-priority tasks.

Troubleshooting Sharing and Version Control

1. Unintended Changes

- Check the activity log to identify who made the change.
- Restore the previous version if necessary.

2. Access Issues

- Ensure collaborators have accepted their invitations.
- Verify their permissions in the **Share** menu.

3. Version Confusion

- Use comments to clarify updates or discrepancies.
- Consolidate multiple versions into a single, accurate sheet.

Real-World Applications

Example 1: Project Management

- Share your project plan with editors and stakeholders.
- Use locked rows for milestones to prevent accidental edits.

Example 2: Budget Tracking

- Restrict admin access to the finance team.
- Create a backup copy of the sheet at the end of each month.

Example 3: Event Planning

- Share the event schedule with vendors and clients as Viewers.
- Use automation to notify team members of updates to the schedule.

Wrapping Up

Sharing and version control are foundational to successful project management in Smartsheet. By following these best practices, you can ensure secure collaboration, maintain data integrity, and streamline workflows.

Section 4:
Task Management and Scheduling

Creating Tasks and Setting Priorities

Effective task management is the cornerstone of project success. By creating and prioritizing tasks in Smartsheet, you can ensure that your team focuses on the right activities at the right time. This chapter will guide you through the process of creating tasks, defining their details, and setting priorities to maximize productivity and efficiency.

Why Task Management Matters

Task management helps you:

1. **Clarify Objectives**: Define clear, actionable steps toward project goals.
2. **Improve Accountability**: Assign tasks and responsibilities to the right team members.
3. **Optimize Resources**: Focus on high-priority tasks to meet deadlines and allocate resources effectively.

Creating Tasks in Smartsheet

1. Define Your Sheet Structure

Before adding tasks, ensure your sheet is structured to support task tracking:

- Include columns for key details such as task name, assigned to, start date, end date, status, and priority.
- Add additional columns as needed for specific project requirements, such as estimated hours or dependencies.

2. Add Tasks to Your Sheet

To create tasks:

1. Open your project sheet in **Grid View**.
2. Add a new row for each task.
3. Enter a clear and descriptive task name in the **Primary Column**.

3. Assign Tasks to Team Members

- Use a **Contact List Column** to assign tasks to specific team members.
- Ensure all assigned team members have access to the sheet.
- Use **@mentions** in the comments section to notify team members about their assignments.

4. Set Deadlines

- Use **Start Date** and **End Date** columns to define task timelines.
- Ensure deadlines are realistic and align with project milestones.

5. Add Context to Tasks

- Attach relevant files or add comments to provide additional details.
  - Example: Attach design mockups for a task related to website development.

Setting Priorities

1. Why Prioritization is Important

Prioritizing tasks helps your team:

- Focus on what matters most.
- Allocate resources efficiently.
- Avoid wasting time on low-impact activities.

2. Using a Priority Column

- Add a **Dropdown Column** to classify task priorities (e.g., High, Medium, Low).
- Use consistent criteria for assigning priorities to ensure fairness and clarity.

3. Highlighting High-Priority Tasks

- Apply **Conditional Formatting** to visually distinguish high-priority tasks.
  - Example: Highlight rows with "High Priority" in red or bold text.

4. Reassessing Priorities

- Regularly review and adjust task priorities as project conditions change.
  - Example: Elevate a medium-priority task to high priority if a deadline shifts.

Organizing Tasks

1. Grouping Tasks

- Indent subtasks under parent tasks to create a hierarchy.
  - Example: Group tasks for different project phases (e.g., Planning, Execution, Review).
- Use **Card View** to visualize and manage tasks by status or category.

2. Sorting Tasks by Priority

- Sort your sheet by the **Priority Column** to display high-priority tasks at the top.
- Combine sorting with filters to focus on tasks assigned to a specific team member or due within a certain timeframe.

3. Using Gantt Charts for Timeline Planning

- Switch to **Gantt Chart View** to visualize task dependencies and timelines.
- Adjust start and end dates to ensure high-priority tasks are scheduled appropriately.

Monitoring Task Progress

1. Status Tracking

- Add a **Dropdown Column** for task status (e.g., Not Started, In Progress, Completed).
- Update task statuses regularly to reflect progress.

2. Using Dashboards

- Create a dashboard to monitor task completion rates and highlight overdue tasks.
- Use widgets to display key metrics such as the percentage of high-priority tasks completed.

3. Setting Up Notifications

- Use automation rules to notify team members of upcoming deadlines or status changes.
  - Example: Send reminders for high-priority tasks due within 48 hours.

Real-World Applications

Example 1: Product Development

- Break down the development process into tasks such as "Requirement Gathering," "Design," "Testing," and "Launch."
- Assign priorities based on the criticality of each task to the overall timeline.

Example 2: Marketing Campaigns

- Use priority settings to focus on high-impact tasks like "Ad Creative Development" and "Audience Targeting."
- Monitor task completion to ensure deadlines for campaign launch are met.

Example 3: Event Planning

- Create tasks for key activities like "Venue Booking," "Catering Arrangements," and "Guest Invitations."
- Assign high priority to tasks with strict deadlines, such as printing materials for the event.

Pro Tips for Task Management

1. **Break Down Large Tasks**
   - Divide complex tasks into smaller, manageable subtasks to avoid overwhelm.
2. **Review Tasks Daily**
   - Regularly review and update tasks to keep your project on track.
3. **Use Filters for Focused Views**
   - Filter tasks by team member, status, or priority to focus on what matters most.
4. **Automate Reminders**
   - Set up automated reminders for overdue tasks to maintain momentum.

Wrapping Up

Creating tasks and setting priorities in Smartsheet lays the foundation for effective project management. By organizing and focusing on the most critical activities, you can drive your project toward success while keeping your team aligned and motivated.

Managing Dependencies and Milestones

Effective project management requires understanding how tasks relate to one another and ensuring key milestones are met. Smartsheet's dependency and milestone features allow you to create dynamic project schedules, track progress, and adapt to changes efficiently. This chapter provides a comprehensive guide to managing dependencies and milestones in Smartsheet.

Understanding Dependencies and Milestones

Dependencies

Dependencies indicate how tasks are connected, helping you visualize and manage their relationships.

- **Types of Dependencies**:
  - **Finish-to-Start**: One task must finish before another can start.
  - **Start-to-Start**: Two tasks must begin simultaneously.
  - **Finish-to-Finish**: Two tasks must conclude at the same time.
  - **Start-to-Finish**: Rarely used, one task's start dictates another's finish.

Milestones

Milestones are significant points in a project, such as deadlines or the completion of critical tasks.

- Milestones typically have zero duration and are used to mark important project achievements.

Setting Up Dependencies

1. Enable Dependencies in Your Sheet

- Open your project sheet and click **Project Settings** in the toolbar.
- Toggle on **Dependencies Enabled** to activate the dependency and predecessor columns.

2. Add the Predecessor Column

- A **Predecessor Column** will appear in your sheet once dependencies are enabled.
- Use this column to link tasks by entering the row number of the preceding task.

3. Define Task Relationships

- Specify the dependency type and lag time (if any) in the **Predecessor Column**.
  - **Lag Time**: Adds a delay between tasks (e.g., Task B starts 2 days after Task A finishes).
  - **Lead Time**: Allows overlapping tasks (e.g., Task B starts 2 days before Task A finishes).

Visualizing Dependencies with Gantt Charts

Smartsheet's Gantt Chart View makes it easy to visualize dependencies:

1. Switch to **Gantt Chart View** using the toolbar.
2. Linked tasks will display connecting lines, illustrating their relationships.
3. Drag and drop task bars to adjust dates and automatically update dependencies.

Managing Milestones

1. Create Milestones in Your Sheet

- Add a milestone by creating a task with a **Start Date** and **End Date** that are the same.
- Set the task duration to zero to mark it as a milestone.

2. Highlight Milestones in Gantt Charts

- Milestones appear as diamonds in Gantt Chart View.
- Use color coding to differentiate milestones from regular tasks.

3. Track Milestone Completion

- Add a **Status Column** to indicate milestone progress (e.g., Not Started, In Progress, Completed).

Best Practices for Managing Dependencies and Milestones

1. Plan Dependencies Early

- Define task relationships during the project planning phase to avoid scheduling conflicts later.

2. Regularly Review Dependencies

- Monitor dependencies throughout the project to ensure they remain valid as tasks are updated.

3. Avoid Overcomplicating Dependencies

- Keep task relationships simple to maintain clarity.
- Use a combination of dependencies and manual scheduling for flexibility.

4. Communicate Milestones Clearly

- Share milestone dates with your team and stakeholders to ensure alignment.
- Use Smartsheet's sharing features to provide real-time visibility into milestone progress.

Troubleshooting Dependencies and Milestones

1. Task Dates Are Not Updating Automatically

- Ensure dependencies are enabled in **Project Settings**.
- Check for circular references in the **Predecessor Column** (e.g., Task A depends on Task B, and Task B depends on Task A).

2. Conflicting Dependencies

- Resolve conflicts by reviewing the task sequence and adjusting predecessor values.

3. Missed Milestones

- Use conditional formatting to highlight overdue milestones in red.
- Set up alerts to notify team members when milestone dates approach.

Real-World Applications

Example 1: Product Launch

- Use dependencies to link tasks like "Finalize Design," "Create Marketing Materials," and "Launch Campaign."
- Add milestones for key events, such as "Product Launch Day" or "Press Release Sent."

Example 2: Construction Projects

- Manage dependencies for phases such as "Site Preparation," "Foundation Work," and "Structural Assembly."
- Include milestones for project inspections or approvals.

Example 3: Event Planning

- Link tasks for vendor coordination, venue setup, and guest invitations.
- Add milestones for key dates, such as "Event Date" or "Registration Deadline."

Pro Tips for Managing Dependencies and Milestones

1. **Use Automation**
   - Create alerts to notify team members of task or milestone updates.
2. **Leverage Dashboards**
   - Track milestone progress and dependency updates visually using Smartsheet dashboards.
3. **Iterate and Adjust**
   - Reassess dependencies and milestones regularly to account for project changes.

Wrapping Up

Managing dependencies and milestones effectively is critical for keeping your project on schedule and aligned with its goals. By leveraging Smartsheet's features, you can visualize task relationships, monitor progress, and adapt to changes with confidence.

Using Gantt Charts for Timeline Visualization

Gantt charts are a cornerstone of effective project management, offering a clear visual representation of your project timeline, task dependencies, and milestones. Smartsheet makes it simple to create and manage Gantt charts, enabling teams to track progress and stay aligned. This chapter walks you through the process of using Gantt charts in Smartsheet to optimize your project timelines.

What is a Gantt Chart?

A Gantt chart is a visual tool used to:

- Display tasks as horizontal bars across a timeline.
- Illustrate task durations, start and end dates, and dependencies.
- Highlight critical milestones and overall project progress.

Benefits of Using Gantt Charts in Smartsheet

1. **Visual Clarity**: See the entire project at a glance.
2. **Dependency Tracking**: Manage relationships between tasks.
3. **Timeline Adjustments**: Easily update schedules to adapt to changes.
4. **Progress Monitoring**: Track task completion against deadlines.

Creating a Gantt Chart in Smartsheet

1. Set Up Your Sheet

Before enabling Gantt chart view:

- Ensure your sheet has **Start Date** and **End Date** columns.
- Add a **Duration Column** to calculate task lengths if needed.
- Include a **Predecessor Column** to establish dependencies (optional).

2. Enable Gantt Chart View

1. Open your project sheet.
2. Click the **Gantt View** button in the toolbar.
3. Your tasks will automatically display as horizontal bars on the timeline based on their start and end dates.

3. Customize the Timeline

- Use the **Zoom Tool** to adjust the timeline scale (e.g., days, weeks, months).
- Drag task bars directly in the Gantt chart to adjust dates dynamically.

Adding Dependencies in Gantt Charts

1. Enable Dependencies

- Go to **Project Settings** and enable **Dependencies**.
- This will activate the Predecessor Column, allowing you to link tasks.

2. Link Tasks

- In the **Predecessor Column**, enter the row number of the preceding task.
- Specify the type of dependency (e.g., Finish-to-Start).
- Smartsheet will automatically update task relationships and timelines.

3. Visualizing Dependencies

- Dependencies appear as lines connecting task bars in the Gantt chart.
- Use these lines to identify critical task relationships and adjust as needed.

Highlighting Milestones

1. Define Milestones

- Create a task with a **Start Date** and **End Date** that are the same.
- Set the **Duration** to zero to convert the task into a milestone.

2. Visualizing Milestones

- Milestones appear as diamonds in the Gantt chart.
- Use different colors or symbols to distinguish milestones from regular tasks.

Customizing Your Gantt Chart

1. Adjust Task Bar Colors

- Right-click on task bars to change their color for better visualization.
- Use colors to differentiate between task categories, teams, or priorities.

2. Add Conditional Formatting

- Highlight tasks based on status, priority, or other criteria.
  - Example: Apply a red background to overdue tasks.

3. Include Additional Details

- Add columns for notes, resources, or task owners to display more information alongside the Gantt chart.

Monitoring and Updating Timelines

1. Track Progress

- Add a **Status Column** (e.g., Not Started, In Progress, Completed).
- Update statuses regularly to reflect progress in the Gantt chart.

2. Adjust Schedules

- Drag task bars or dependency lines to reschedule tasks dynamically.
- Smartsheet will automatically update linked tasks and durations.

3. Use Dashboards for Insights

- Create dashboards to display Gantt chart summaries, progress metrics, and key milestones for stakeholders.

Best Practices for Using Gantt Charts

1. **Plan Dependencies Early**
   - Define task relationships at the start to avoid schedule conflicts.
2. **Keep It Simple**
   - Avoid overloading the Gantt chart with unnecessary details. Focus on key tasks and milestones.
3. **Communicate Changes**
   - Notify team members of timeline adjustments to maintain alignment.
4. **Use Filters for Focused Views**
   - Filter tasks by owner, status, or priority to focus on specific parts of the project.

Real-World Applications

Example 1: Software Development

- Use Gantt charts to track sprints, task dependencies, and release dates.
- Highlight critical milestones like "Beta Launch" and "Final Deployment."

Example 2: Marketing Campaigns

- Visualize campaign phases such as planning, execution, and analysis.
- Use dependencies to link creative development tasks to final approvals.

Example 3: Event Planning

- Track vendor coordination, venue setup, and guest management.
- Add milestones for key deadlines like "Invitations Sent" and "Event Day."

Troubleshooting Common Issues

1. Tasks Not Appearing in Gantt View

- Ensure tasks have valid start and end dates.
- Check for circular dependencies in the Predecessor Column.

2. Overlapping Dependencies

- Review dependency lines in the Gantt chart and adjust task schedules to resolve conflicts.

3. Difficulty Reading the Timeline

- Use the zoom tool to adjust the scale or focus on specific date ranges.

Wrapping Up: Gantt charts in Smartsheet provide a powerful way to visualize and manage your project timelines. By mastering their setup and customization, you can ensure that your team stays on track and meets critical milestones.

Automating Reminders and Alerts

Automation is a powerful feature in Smartsheet that helps ensure tasks are completed on time, deadlines are not missed, and team members stay informed. By automating reminders and alerts, you can enhance task management, improve productivity, and reduce manual follow-ups. In this chapter, we'll explore how to set up and use automated reminders and alerts in Smartsheet effectively.

Why Automate Reminders and Alerts?

Automating reminders and alerts offers several benefits:

1. **Save Time**: Eliminate manual follow-ups and reduce administrative effort.
2. **Increase Accountability**: Ensure team members are aware of their responsibilities.
3. **Enhance Collaboration**: Keep everyone informed about updates and changes.
4. **Minimize Errors**: Reduce the risk of missed deadlines or overlooked tasks.

Key Features for Automation

Smartsheet provides a robust set of tools to automate notifications and reminders:

1. Alerts

Alerts notify users of changes to specific rows, such as updates to task status or priority.

2. Reminders

Reminders are sent to users at a specified time or interval, ensuring they complete tasks or address deadlines.

3. Approval Requests

Automated approval workflows send requests to designated users for review or confirmation.

4. Recurring Workflows

Set up recurring notifications or reminders for ongoing tasks, such as weekly updates.

Setting Up Automated Alerts

1. Basic Alerts

1. Open your sheet and click **Automation > Create a Workflow**.
2. Choose **Alert Someone** from the workflow options.
3. Define the trigger for the alert:
   - Example: "When a row is updated" or "When a due date changes."
4. Specify the recipients:
   - Choose individuals, contact groups, or dynamic fields like "Assigned To."
5. Customize the message:
   - Include relevant details such as task name, due date, or priority.

2. Condition-Based Alerts

- Add conditions to your alert workflow to trigger notifications only under specific circumstances.
  - Example: Notify the project manager only when the task status changes to "Overdue."

Setting Up Automated Reminders

1. Due Date Reminders

1. Go to **Automation > Create a Workflow** and select **Set a Reminder**.
2. Define the trigger:
   - Example: "X days before the due date."
3. Select recipients:
   - Notify the task owner or other stakeholders.
4. Customize the reminder message:
   - Example: "Reminder: The task '[Task Name]' is due on [Due Date]."

2. Recurring Reminders

- Use recurring workflows for tasks that repeat over time.
  - Example: Send a weekly reminder to update progress on tasks.

Customizing Notifications

Smartsheet allows you to tailor notifications to fit your needs:

1. Email Notifications

- Notifications are sent via email with detailed information about the trigger.
- Ensure users' email addresses are up to date in Smartsheet.

2. In-App Notifications

- Recipients can view alerts and reminders directly in Smartsheet under the **Notification Center**.

3. Mobile Push Notifications

- For users with the Smartsheet mobile app, push notifications provide real-time updates.

Managing and Tracking Automation

1. Monitor Workflows

- View and manage all automation rules in the **Automation Center**.
- Check the status of workflows and troubleshoot errors if necessary.

2. Audit Automation Logs

- Use the automation log to review past notifications and ensure workflows are functioning as intended.

3. Test Workflows

- Run a test workflow before activating it to confirm that notifications and reminders are working correctly.

Best Practices for Automating Reminders and Alerts

1. **Be Specific with Triggers**
   - Use precise conditions to avoid unnecessary notifications.
   - Example: Notify the project manager only when the task is marked as "Delayed."
2. **Keep Messages Clear**
   - Include all relevant details in notifications to minimize follow-ups.
3. **Avoid Overloading Users**
   - Limit the frequency of alerts to prevent recipients from ignoring notifications.
4. **Combine Automation with Filters**
   - Use filters to narrow down tasks and create focused workflows.
5. **Regularly Review Workflows**
   - Audit workflows periodically to ensure they remain relevant and effective.

Real-World Applications

Example 1: Project Deadlines

- Automate reminders to notify team members 48 hours before a task's due date.
- Send alerts to the project manager when a task status changes to "At Risk."

Example 2: Approval Processes

- Set up approval requests for budget updates or milestone sign-offs.
- Notify approvers and track responses within Smartsheet.

Example 3: Task Updates

- Use recurring alerts to remind team members to update task progress every Friday.

Troubleshooting Common Issues

1. Recipients Not Receiving Notifications

- Ensure the correct email addresses are assigned to the "Assigned To" field.
- Check spam or junk folders for missed emails.

2. Automation Not Triggering

- Verify that all conditions in the workflow are met.
- Check the automation log for errors.

3. Duplicate Notifications

- Combine workflows or adjust conditions to avoid overlapping triggers.

Wrapping Up

Automating reminders and alerts in Smartsheet is a game-changer for task management, ensuring that everyone stays on track and critical deadlines are met. By implementing these automation techniques, you can reduce manual effort, improve communication, and drive project success.

Section 5:
Formulas, Functions, and Formatting

Writing Basic Formulas in Smartsheet

Formulas are a powerful feature in Smartsheet, allowing you to perform calculations, analyze data, and create dynamic content within your sheets. Writing basic formulas is an essential skill for managing projects effectively. In this chapter, we'll cover the fundamentals of creating and using formulas in Smartsheet, empowering you to harness the full potential of your data.

Understanding Formulas in Smartsheet

What Are Formulas?

Formulas in Smartsheet are used to calculate values, manipulate text, and analyze data based on the information in your sheet. Similar to spreadsheet software like Excel, Smartsheet formulas can reference cells, rows, or columns.

Key Features of Smartsheet Formulas

1. **Cross-Column Calculations**: Combine data from multiple columns.
2. **Dynamic Updates**: Automatically recalculate when data changes.
3. **Consistency**: Ensure uniform calculations across your sheet.

Basic Formula Syntax

Smartsheet formulas always start with an equals sign (**=**). The basic structure is:

```
=FunctionName([Column Name]@row, [Additional Arguments])
```

Key Elements of Formula Syntax

1. **FunctionName**: The specific operation you want to perform (e.g., SUM, IF).
2. **[Column Name]**: The name of the column you want to reference.
3. **@row**: Refers to the current row where the formula is applied.

Writing Basic Formulas

1. Performing Arithmetic Operations

Use formulas to perform calculations like addition, subtraction, multiplication, and division.

- **Example**: Calculate total cost by multiplying quantity and price.

```
=[Quantity]@row * [Price]@row
```

2. Using the SUM Function

The SUM function adds up values in a column or range.

- **Example**: Calculate the total budget for a project.

  `=SUM([Budget]:[Budget])`

3. Creating Conditional Logic with IF

The IF function allows you to apply logic based on specific conditions.

- **Example**: Mark tasks as overdue if today's date is past the due date.

  `=IF([Due Date]@row < TODAY(), "Overdue", "On Track")`

4. Counting Values with COUNT

The COUNT function counts the number of entries in a column or range.

- **Example**: Count the number of completed tasks.

  `=COUNTIF([Status]:[Status], "Complete")`

5. Joining Text with CONCATENATE

Combine text from multiple columns into one cell.

- **Example**: Create a full name by combining first and last names.

  `=CONCATENATE([First Name]@row, " ", [Last Name]@row)`

Referencing Data

1. Column References

- Reference an entire column to include all rows.

  `=SUM([Revenue]:[Revenue])`

2. Row References

- Use **@row** to reference the current row.

  `=[Hours Worked]@row * [Hourly Rate]@row`

3. Absolute References

- Use absolute references to lock specific cells or ranges.

  `=SUM($[Fixed Cost]$1:$[Fixed Cost]$5)`

Formatting Formula Results

1. Number Formatting

- Apply number formatting (e.g., currency, percentage) to display results appropriately.
  - Example: Format the result of a formula calculating profit as currency.

2. Conditional Formatting

- Highlight formula results based on conditions.
  - Example: Apply red formatting to cells where budget exceeds limits.

Troubleshooting Formulas

1. Error Messages

- **#INVALID REF**: The column or cell reference is incorrect.
- **#DIV/0!**: Division by zero.
- **#UNPARSEABLE**: Syntax error in the formula.

2. Testing Formulas

- Test your formula on a small dataset before applying it to the entire sheet.

3. Debugging Tips

- Check column names and ensure they match the formula references.
- Use parentheses to clarify the order of operations.

Practical Applications

Example 1: Budget Tracking

- Calculate total project expenses by summing up costs from different tasks.

```
=SUM([Task Cost]:[Task Cost])
```

Example 2: Task Progress Monitoring

- Use an IF formula to flag overdue tasks.

```
=IF([Due Date]@row < TODAY(), "Overdue", "On Track")
```

Example 3: Sales Reporting

- Combine product names and regions for detailed sales reports.

```
=CONCATENATE([Product]@row, " - ", [Region]@row)
```

Pro Tips for Writing Formulas

1. **Use Clear Column Names**
   - Name columns descriptively to simplify formula writing.
2. **Leverage the Formula Help Tool**

- ○ Use Smartsheet's formula builder to access function guides and examples.
3. **Start Simple**
    - ○ Build complex formulas incrementally to ensure accuracy.
4. **Keep Formulas Consistent**
    - ○ Apply the same formula structure across related columns or rows for uniformity.

Wrapping Up

Writing basic formulas in Smartsheet empowers you to analyze data, automate calculations, and gain insights from your projects. By mastering these foundational techniques, you can create more dynamic and functional sheets that drive project success.

Applying Advanced Functions

Mastering advanced functions in Smartsheet can significantly enhance your ability to analyze data, automate processes, and create dynamic workflows. This chapter explores powerful functions and how to apply them effectively, providing you with tools to tackle complex scenarios and streamline your projects.

Why Use Advanced Functions?

Advanced functions allow you to:

1. **Simplify Complex Calculations**: Perform intricate operations without manual intervention.
2. **Analyze Data Effectively**: Extract insights from large datasets.
3. **Automate Workflows**: Reduce repetitive tasks and save time.

Overview of Advanced Functions

1. IF and Nested IF Statements

The IF function evaluates conditions and returns specific results. Nesting IF statements adds complexity.

- **Example**: Assign priority levels based on task deadlines.

  ```
  =IF([Due Date]@row < TODAY(), "High", IF([Due Date]@row <= TODAY() + 7,
  "Medium", "Low"))
  ```

2. COUNTIF and SUMIF

These conditional functions allow you to count or sum values that meet specific criteria.

- **COUNTIF Example**: Count tasks marked as "Complete."

  ```
  =COUNTIF([Status]:[Status], "Complete")
  ```

- **SUMIF Example**: Sum budgets for tasks in the "Marketing" category.

  ```
  =SUMIF([Category]:[Category], "Marketing", [Budget]:[Budget])
  ```

3. VLOOKUP

Search for a value in a column and return a corresponding value from another column.

- **Example**: Look up a project's manager based on its ID.

  ```
  =VLOOKUP([Project ID]@row, {Project Data}, 2, false)
  ```

4. INDEX and MATCH

These functions are used together for flexible data lookup and retrieval.

- **Example**: Retrieve a task's due date based on its name.

  ```
  =INDEX([Due Date]:[Due Date], MATCH("Task Name", [Task Name]:[Task Name], 0))
  ```

5. CONTAINS

Check if a column or range contains a specific value.

- **Example**: Identify rows that include the keyword "Urgent."

```
=IF(CONTAINS("Urgent", [Notes]@row), "Yes", "No")
```

Leveraging Date and Time Functions

1. TODAY and NOW

- **TODAY**: Returns the current date.

```
=TODAY()
```

- **NOW**: Returns the current date and time.

```
=NOW()
```

2. DATE and YEAR Functions

- Create custom date values or extract specific components.
  - **Example**: Combine year, month, and day columns into a single date.

```
=DATE([Year]@row, [Month]@row, [Day]@row)
```

3. WORKDAY

- Calculate deadlines while excluding weekends and holidays.
  - **Example**: Determine a task's due date after 10 workdays.

```
=WORKDAY([Start Date]@row, 10, {Holiday Dates})
```

Text Manipulation Functions

1. LEFT, RIGHT, and MID

Extract parts of a text string.

- **Example**: Extract the first three letters of a project code.

```
=LEFT([Project Code]@row, 3)
```

2. FIND

Locate the position of a substring within a text string.

- **Example**: Find the position of "@" in an email address.

```
=FIND("@", [Email]@row)
```

3. LEN and SUBSTITUTE

Measure text length and replace specific text.

- **Example**: Count characters in a task name and replace "Task" with "Job."

```
=LEN([Task Name]@row)
=SUBSTITUTE([Task Name]@row, "Task", "Job")
```

Logical Functions for Advanced Automation

1. AND and OR

Combine multiple conditions in a formula.

- **Example**: Flag tasks that are both overdue and high priority.

```
=IF(AND([Due Date]@row < TODAY(), [Priority]@row = "High"), "Critical",
"Normal")
```

2. ISBLANK and ISNUMBER

Check if a cell is empty or contains a number.

- **Example**: Verify if a budget field is missing.

```
=IF(ISBLANK([Budget]@row), "Missing Data", "Complete")
```

Cross-Sheet References

1. Using Cell Linking

- Link data between sheets for real-time updates.
  - Example: Reference a total budget from another sheet.

2. Advanced Cross-Sheet Functions

- Use cross-sheet formulas with references to combine data from multiple sources.
  - Example: Aggregate total hours worked across departments.

```
=SUM({Department Hours})
```

Troubleshooting and Best Practices

Common Errors and Fixes

1. **#UNPARSEABLE**: Check for syntax errors or missing parentheses.
2. **#INVALID REF**: Verify column names and references.
3. **#DIV/0!**: Avoid dividing by zero or blank cells.

Best Practices

1. **Plan Your Formula Structure**: Map out your formula logic before implementation.
2. **Use Descriptive Column Names**: Simplify references by naming columns intuitively.

3. **Test on Small Datasets**: Validate formulas with test data before applying them broadly.

Practical Applications

Example 1: Financial Analysis

- Calculate monthly expenses, revenue, and profit margins.

```
=[Revenue]@row - [Expenses]@row
```

Example 2: Task Monitoring

- Flag tasks due within the next three days.

```
=IF([Due Date]@row <= TODAY() + 3, "Upcoming", "On Schedule")
```

Example 3: Employee Tracking

- Identify employees with missing contact information.

```
=IF(OR(ISBLANK([Email]@row), ISBLANK([Phone]@row)), "Incomplete", "Complete")
```

Wrapping Up

Applying advanced functions in Smartsheet opens up a world of possibilities for data management, automation, and analysis. With these tools, you can handle complex scenarios with ease and drive more effective project outcomes.

Conditional Formatting for Visual Cues

Conditional formatting is a powerful feature in Smartsheet that enhances data visualization by applying colors, icons, or text styles to cells based on specific conditions. This feature makes it easier to identify key trends, prioritize tasks, and monitor project progress at a glance. In this chapter, we'll explore how to set up and effectively use conditional formatting for visual cues in Smartsheet.

Why Use Conditional Formatting?

Conditional formatting allows you to:

1. **Highlight Important Data**: Draw attention to critical tasks, milestones, or deadlines.
2. **Enhance Decision-Making**: Quickly identify bottlenecks or risks in a project.
3. **Improve Clarity**: Simplify large datasets by visually categorizing data.
4. **Boost Efficiency**: Reduce the time spent manually reviewing and interpreting data.

Setting Up Conditional Formatting

1. Accessing the Conditional Formatting Tool

- Open your Smartsheet.
- Click on **Conditional Formatting** in the toolbar to open the formatting rules panel.

2. Creating a New Rule

1. Click **+ New Rule** in the formatting panel.
2. Define the criteria for the rule:
    - **Apply to**: Choose the column(s) or the entire sheet where the rule will apply.
    - **Condition**: Specify the logic for the rule (e.g., "Status is Completed").
3. Select the formatting options:
    - Change the cell or text color, add bold or italic text, or use icons for emphasis.
4. Click **OK** to save the rule.

Common Use Cases for Conditional Formatting

1. Highlighting Overdue Tasks

- **Rule**: Apply red text or background to tasks where the due date is earlier than today's date.

    ```
    Condition: [Due Date] is before TODAY()
    ```

2. Flagging High-Priority Tasks

- **Rule**: Use bold text or a bright background color for tasks with "High" priority.

    ```
    Condition: [Priority] is equal to "High"
    ```

3. Tracking Status Progress

- **Rule**: Assign different colors for each task status (e.g., Green for "Completed," Yellow for "In Progress," Red for "Not Started").

  ```
  Condition: [Status] is equal to "Completed"
  ```

4. Monitoring Budget Thresholds

- **Rule**: Highlight cells where the budget exceeds a predefined limit.

  ```
  Condition: [Budget] is greater than 10000
  ```

5. Identifying Missing Data

- **Rule**: Flag cells that are blank with a specific background color.

  ```
  Condition: [Assigned To] is blank
  ```

Customizing Conditional Formatting

1. Using Multiple Conditions

- Combine multiple criteria in one rule.
  - **Example**: Highlight overdue tasks that are also marked as "High Priority."

    ```
    Condition 1: [Due Date] is before TODAY()
    Condition 2: [Priority] is equal to "High"
    ```

2. Layering Rules

- Apply multiple rules to the same cells.
  - **Example**: Use a red background for overdue tasks and bold text for high-priority items.

3. Copying and Reusing Rules

- Duplicate existing rules and modify them for similar columns or conditions.

Best Practices for Conditional Formatting

1. **Keep It Simple**
   - Avoid overloading your sheet with too many rules to maintain clarity.
2. **Use Consistent Colors**
   - Apply a standard color scheme for similar conditions across sheets.
   - **Example**: Use red for overdue items, green for completed tasks, and yellow for in-progress tasks.
3. **Test Your Rules**
   - Apply the rules to a sample dataset to ensure they work as intended before scaling up.
4. **Document Formatting Logic**
   - Include a legend or key to explain the meaning of colors or styles, especially for shared sheets.
5. **Update Rules Regularly**
   - Review and refine formatting rules as project requirements evolve.

Real-World Applications

Example 1: Task Management

- Highlight overdue tasks, in-progress tasks, and completed tasks with distinct colors to track progress visually.

Example 2: Budget Monitoring

- Use conditional formatting to flag budgets exceeding a certain percentage of the total allocation.

Example 3: Employee Performance Tracking

- Highlight top-performing employees based on key performance indicators (KPIs).

Example 4: Sales Reporting

- Differentiate high-value deals from smaller ones using bold text or icons.

Troubleshooting Conditional Formatting

1. Rules Not Applying Correctly

- Ensure that column names match the references in your conditions.
- Verify that the data type (e.g., date, text, number) matches the rule criteria.

2. Conflicting Rules

- Arrange rules in the correct priority order to avoid overlap.
- Combine related conditions into a single rule when possible.

3. Performance Issues

- Too many rules can slow down your sheet. Consolidate or simplify rules where possible.

Wrapping Up

Conditional formatting transforms your Smartsheet into a visually intuitive tool, making it easier to interpret and act on your data. By using these techniques, you can highlight critical information, enhance decision-making, and ensure your team stays aligned with project priorities.

Linking Data Across Multiple Sheets

In complex projects, data is often spread across multiple sheets. Smartsheet's cross-sheet linking feature enables you to consolidate and synchronize data from different sheets, creating a centralized hub for better project management and reporting. This chapter provides a comprehensive guide to linking data across multiple sheets, helping you streamline workflows and improve decision-making.

Why Link Data Across Sheets?

Cross-sheet linking offers several benefits:

1. **Centralized Information**: Combine data from multiple sheets into one view for easy access.
2. **Improved Accuracy**: Avoid manual updates by dynamically syncing data.
3. **Enhanced Reporting**: Build reports and dashboards using data from various sources.
4. **Seamless Collaboration**: Share consolidated data with stakeholders without duplicating work.

Understanding Cross-Sheet Linking

Key Concepts

- **Cell Linking**: Establishes a direct connection between specific cells in different sheets.
- **Reference Data**: Pulls information from a source sheet to a destination sheet.

Use Cases

- Consolidating budgets from multiple project sheets into a single financial overview.
- Creating a master task tracker by pulling data from individual team sheets.
- Generating summaries for stakeholders without exposing detailed sheets.

Setting Up Cross-Sheet Links

1. Preparing the Source and Destination Sheets

- Identify the **source sheet** containing the data you want to link.
- Create or open the **destination sheet** where the data will appear.

2. Creating a Cell Link

1. In the destination sheet, click on the cell where you want the data to appear.
2. Select **Insert > Link from Cell in Other Sheet** from the toolbar.
3. Navigate to the source sheet in the pop-up window.
4. Click on the cell you want to link and confirm the selection.

3. Using Cross-Sheet Formulas

- Reference entire ranges or columns using cross-sheet formulas.
  - **Example**: Calculate the total budget from multiple sheets.

    ```
    =SUM({Sheet1 Budget}, {Sheet2 Budget})
    ```

Advanced Techniques for Cross-Sheet Linking

1. Using Named Ranges

- Assign descriptive names to linked ranges for easier reference in formulas.
    - **Example**: Use `{Marketing Expenses}` instead of a raw range reference.

2. Combining Data with Aggregation Functions

- Aggregate data from multiple sheets using functions like SUM, COUNT, or AVERAGE.
    - **Example**: Calculate the total hours worked across teams.

```
=SUM({Team A Hours}, {Team B Hours})
```

3. Dynamic Linking with Criteria

- Use conditional functions like SUMIF or COUNTIF with cross-sheet references.
    - **Example**: Sum expenses for a specific category across sheets.

```
=SUMIF({Expense Category}, "Travel", {Expense Amount})
```

4. Error Handling

- Use error-checking functions to handle missing or invalid links.
    - **Example**:

```
=IFERROR(SUM({Budget}), "Data Not Available")
```

Maintaining Linked Data

1. Refreshing Links

- Links update automatically, but ensure users have access to source sheets for smooth updates.

2. Managing Access Permissions

- Confirm that collaborators have appropriate access to both source and destination sheets.
    - **Tip**: Use "Viewer" access for stakeholders who only need to see the linked data.

3. Tracking Changes

- Use the **Cell History** feature to review updates to linked cells.

Common Challenges and Solutions

1. Broken Links

- **Cause**: Source data has been deleted or moved.
- **Solution**: Recreate the link or restore the source data.

2. Access Issues

- **Cause**: Users lack permissions for the source sheet.
- **Solution**: Update sharing permissions or use a shared workspace.

3. Performance Slowdowns

- **Cause**: Excessive links or complex formulas.
- **Solution**: Simplify links and consolidate data before linking.

Best Practices for Cross-Sheet Linking

1. **Plan Your Data Structure**
   - Organize sheets logically to minimize unnecessary links.
2. **Use Descriptive Naming Conventions**
   - Name sheets, columns, and ranges clearly to simplify linking.
3. **Limit the Number of Links**
   - Avoid overloading sheets with excessive links to maintain performance.
4. **Regularly Audit Links**
   - Periodically check for broken or outdated links.
5. **Document Links**
   - Maintain a record of linked sheets for easy troubleshooting and updates.

Real-World Applications

Example 1: Budget Consolidation

- Link budget data from departmental sheets into a master financial sheet.
- Use SUMIF to calculate totals for specific expense categories.

Example 2: Project Portfolio Management

- Create a centralized tracker pulling data from individual project sheets.
- Highlight overdue tasks or milestones using conditional formatting.

Example 3: Resource Allocation

- Link resource availability data from team sheets into a master scheduling sheet.

Example 4: Sales Reporting

- Aggregate sales data from regional sheets into a global performance dashboard.

Wrapping Up

Cross-sheet linking is a game-changing feature in Smartsheet that enables seamless integration of data across multiple sheets. By leveraging this functionality, you can centralize information, enhance reporting, and streamline project workflows.

Section 6:
Reporting and Analytics

Creating Custom Reports for Stakeholders

In project management, effectively communicating progress, risks, and outcomes to stakeholders is crucial. Smartsheet's custom reporting feature allows you to consolidate data from multiple sheets into a tailored report, ensuring stakeholders receive the insights they need. In this chapter, we'll explore how to create custom reports, highlight key metrics, and optimize your reports for clear communication.

Why Use Custom Reports for Stakeholders?

Custom reports enable you to:

1. **Centralize Data**: Gather information from multiple sheets in one place.
2. **Enhance Visibility**: Present tailored insights to stakeholders.
3. **Save Time**: Automate updates, so reports stay current with real-time data.
4. **Simplify Decision-Making**: Provide concise, actionable information.

Types of Reports

1. Row Reports

- Consolidate rows from multiple sheets based on specific criteria.
- Ideal for task tracking, resource allocation, and status updates.

2. Sheet Summary Reports

- Aggregate high-level data from sheet summaries.
- Useful for project overviews, budget summaries, and portfolio management.

Setting Up a Custom Report

1. Create a New Report

1. Navigate to the **Home Tab** in Smartsheet.
2. Click **Create > Report** and select the type of report (Row or Sheet Summary).
3. Name your report and click **OK** to proceed.

2. Define the Data Source

- Choose the sheets you want to pull data from.
- You can select multiple sheets or entire workspaces.

3. Apply Filters

- Use filters to narrow down the data included in your report.
  - **Example**: Only include tasks with a status of "In Progress."

4. Select Columns

- Choose the specific columns to include in your report.
  - Focus on the columns that are most relevant to stakeholders, such as task name, status, and due date.

Customizing the Report

1. Sort and Group Data

- Organize rows by criteria such as priority, status, or assigned team member.
- Use grouping to create clear sections for better readability.

2. Add Conditional Formatting

- Highlight critical data points using conditional formatting.
  - **Example**: Apply a red background to overdue tasks.

3. Incorporate Visual Elements

- Include charts, graphs, or widgets for visual representation.
  - Combine the report with a Smartsheet dashboard for enhanced visualization.

Sharing the Report

1. Collaborate in Real-Time

- Share the report with stakeholders via email or Smartsheet's sharing feature.
- Set permissions to control who can view or edit the report.

2. Export Options

- Export the report as a PDF, Excel, or CSV file for offline sharing.

3. Schedule Automated Updates

- Set up recurring email updates to send the report to stakeholders on a regular schedule.

Best Practices for Custom Reports

1. **Tailor the Report to the Audience**
   - Focus on data that aligns with stakeholder priorities, such as KPIs or risks.
2. **Keep It Concise**
   - Avoid overwhelming stakeholders with unnecessary details. Highlight key metrics and trends.
3. **Use Clear Labels**
   - Ensure column headers and sections are labeled intuitively.
4. **Combine Reports with Dashboards**
   - Link reports to dashboards for a more comprehensive view of the project.

5. **Test and Refine**
   ○ Review the report with stakeholders and adjust based on their feedback.

Real-World Applications

Example 1: Project Progress Report

- Create a row report that consolidates tasks from multiple team sheets.
- Include columns for task name, assigned to, status, and due date.
- Apply filters to exclude completed tasks.

Example 2: Budget Summary Report

- Build a sheet summary report that aggregates budget data from all project sheets.
- Highlight total spend, remaining budget, and overspend risks.

Example 3: Portfolio Overview

- Create a high-level report summarizing key metrics for all active projects.
- Include columns for project name, progress percentage, and milestone completion.

Troubleshooting Common Issues

1. Missing Data in Reports

- **Cause**: The source sheet or data range is not included.
- **Solution**: Verify the sheets and columns selected in the report builder.

2. Outdated Data

- **Cause**: Source sheets are not updated in real-time.
- **Solution**: Ensure collaborators regularly update the source sheets.

3. Excessive Information

- **Cause**: The report includes irrelevant or redundant data.
- **Solution**: Refine filters and columns to focus on critical information.

Wrapping Up

Custom reports are a vital tool for communicating project progress and insights to stakeholders. By tailoring reports to specific needs, incorporating visual elements, and automating updates, you can ensure stakeholders have the information they need to make informed decisions.

Building Interactive Dashboards

Interactive dashboards in Smartsheet provide a centralized, real-time view of project data, enabling stakeholders to track progress, monitor KPIs, and make informed decisions. By leveraging widgets, visual elements, and automated updates, dashboards become a dynamic tool for project success. In this chapter, we'll explore how to design and build interactive dashboards tailored to your project needs.

Why Use Dashboards in Smartsheet?

Dashboards offer several advantages:

1. **Real-Time Insights**: Provide up-to-date project information at a glance.
2. **Enhanced Visibility**: Consolidate data from multiple sources into a single view.
3. **Improved Communication**: Share actionable insights with stakeholders.
4. **Customization**: Tailor dashboards to highlight the most relevant metrics and data.

Components of a Smartsheet Dashboard

1. Widgets

Widgets are the building blocks of dashboards. Types include:

- **Metric Widgets**: Display key numbers like budgets or task counts.
- **Chart Widgets**: Visualize data trends through pie, bar, or line charts.
- **Report Widgets**: Embed live reports to show detailed data.
- **Shortcut Widgets**: Link to sheets, reports, or external resources.
- **Image Widgets**: Add logos, icons, or visual elements.
- **Title Widgets**: Provide headings and context.

2. Data Sources

Dashboards pull data from:

- Sheets
- Reports
- Sheet summaries
- External tools integrated with Smartsheet

Creating an Interactive Dashboard

1. Set Up the Dashboard

1. Go to the **Home Tab** in Smartsheet.
2. Click **Create > Dashboard/Portal**.
3. Name your dashboard and click **OK**.

2. Add Widgets

- Click **Add Widget** and choose the desired widget type.
- Configure each widget by linking it to data sources, setting display options, and applying formatting.

3. Arrange and Design

- Drag and drop widgets to organize the layout.
- Use alignment tools to ensure a clean and professional appearance.

Designing Effective Dashboards

1. Focus on Key Metrics

- Identify the metrics most relevant to your stakeholders.
  - **Example**: Task completion percentage, budget utilization, or project milestones.

2. Use Visual Hierarchy

- Place the most critical data at the top or center of the dashboard.
- Use larger fonts and bold colors for key metrics.

3. Incorporate Visual Elements

- Use charts and graphs to make data easier to interpret.
  - **Example**: Use a bar chart to show progress across multiple phases of a project.

4. Apply Consistent Styling

- Use a consistent color scheme, font style, and widget size to maintain a professional look.

Advanced Features

1. Interactive Elements

- Add filters to allow stakeholders to customize the view.
  - **Example**: Filter data by team, project phase, or date range.

2. Dynamic Updates

- Link widgets to live data sources to ensure the dashboard updates automatically.

3. Embedded Content

- Embed videos, presentations, or external tools for a more comprehensive view.

4. Cross-Dashboard Navigation

- Use shortcut widgets to link multiple dashboards for a seamless navigation experience.

Sharing and Publishing Dashboards

1. Share with Stakeholders

- Click **Share** in the dashboard toolbar.
- Grant view or edit permissions based on the user's role.

2. Publish Dashboards

- Enable **Publish Dashboard** to create a public link for easy sharing.
- Control access with password protection or domain restrictions.

3. Embed Dashboards

- Embed dashboards in external platforms like websites or intranets using an iframe code.

Best Practices for Dashboard Design

1. **Tailor to the Audience**
   - Design dashboards with the specific needs of your stakeholders in mind.
2. **Keep It Simple**
   - Avoid clutter by focusing on essential data and minimizing unnecessary widgets.
3. **Test for Usability**
   - Review the dashboard with a small group of stakeholders before rolling it out.
4. **Update Regularly**
   - Ensure data sources are current and the dashboard remains relevant as project needs evolve.
5. **Provide Context**
   - Include titles, labels, and legends to clarify the meaning of each widget.

Real-World Applications

Example 1: Project Status Dashboard

- Include widgets for task progress, milestone completion, and overdue items.
- Use a pie chart to display task status distribution.

Example 2: Financial Overview Dashboard

- Show total budget, expenses, and remaining funds using metric widgets.
- Embed a report widget for detailed expense tracking.

Example 3: Team Performance Dashboard

- Highlight team member contributions and task completion rates.
- Use a bar chart to compare workloads across teams.

Example 4: Marketing Campaign Dashboard

- Track campaign reach, leads generated, and conversion rates.
- Include shortcut widgets linking to campaign-related sheets and reports.

Troubleshooting Common Issues

1. Data Not Displaying

- **Cause**: Data source is not linked correctly.
- **Solution**: Verify the data source and update widget configurations.

2. Slow Loading

- **Cause**: Excessive widgets or large data sources.
- **Solution**: Optimize the dashboard by reducing the number of widgets or summarizing data.

3. Stakeholder Access Issues

- **Cause**: Permissions not set correctly.
- **Solution**: Check sharing settings and adjust access permissions.

Wrapping Up

Interactive dashboards are an indispensable tool for project management, offering real-time insights and facilitating data-driven decisions. By mastering dashboard creation, you can provide stakeholders with a clear and concise view of project performance, ensuring alignment and transparency.

Tracking KPIs and Metrics

Key Performance Indicators (KPIs) and metrics are essential for measuring project success and ensuring alignment with business goals. Smartsheet provides robust tools to track, analyze, and visualize KPIs and metrics in real time. This chapter will guide you through defining KPIs, setting up tracking mechanisms, and using Smartsheet features to monitor and evaluate performance effectively.

What Are KPIs and Metrics?

Key Performance Indicators (KPIs)

KPIs are measurable values that indicate how effectively an individual, team, or organization is achieving specific objectives.

- **Example**: Percentage of tasks completed on time.

Metrics

Metrics are broader data points that provide context or additional insights into performance.

- **Example**: Total number of active tasks or total project budget.

Why Track KPIs and Metrics?

Tracking KPIs and metrics allows you to:

1. **Measure Progress**: Evaluate how well your project is performing against goals.
2. **Identify Risks**: Detect potential delays or budget overruns early.
3. **Make Informed Decisions**: Base decisions on data rather than assumptions.
4. **Enhance Accountability**: Provide transparency for team members and stakeholders.

Defining KPIs for Your Project

1. Align with Project Goals

- Choose KPIs that directly reflect your project objectives.
  - **Example**: For a marketing campaign, track lead conversion rates.

2. Make KPIs SMART

Ensure that KPIs are:

- **Specific**: Clearly defined and focused.
- **Measurable**: Quantifiable with data.
- **Achievable**: Realistic and attainable.
- **Relevant**: Connected to project goals.
- **Time-Bound**: Include a timeframe for evaluation.

3. Categorize KPIs

- **Efficiency KPIs**: Time to complete tasks, resource utilization.
- **Financial KPIs**: Budget adherence, cost per deliverable.

- **Quality KPIs**: Defect rates, customer satisfaction scores.

Setting Up KPI Tracking in Smartsheet

1. Create a KPI Tracking Sheet

- Design a dedicated sheet with columns for:
  - KPI Name
  - Target Value
  - Current Value
  - Status (e.g., On Track, At Risk, Behind)
  - Owner (responsible person or team)

2. Use Formulas for Calculations

- Calculate performance percentages or variances with formulas.
  - **Example**:

```
=[Current Value]@row / [Target Value]@row * 100
```

3. Apply Conditional Formatting

- Highlight KPIs based on performance thresholds.
  - **Example**:
    - Green: Above 90%
    - Yellow: 70%-89%
    - Red: Below 70%

Visualizing KPIs with Dashboards

1. Add Metric Widgets

- Display key values like total revenue, task completion rates, or average resolution time.

2. Use Chart Widgets

- Visualize trends with bar, line, or pie charts.
  - **Example**: Show task completion rates over time.

3. Embed Live Reports

- Pull data directly from your KPI tracking sheet into a dashboard for real-time updates.

Automating KPI Monitoring

1. Set Up Alerts and Notifications

- Notify team members when KPIs fall below target thresholds.
  - **Example**: Send an alert if the budget utilization exceeds 90%.

2. Leverage Workflows

- Automate status updates or escalate issues based on KPI performance.

Best Practices for Tracking KPIs

1. **Regularly Update Data**
   - Ensure that KPI tracking sheets and dashboards are updated in real time.
2. **Focus on Actionable Insights**
   - Track only the metrics that directly influence decision-making.
3. **Review and Adjust KPIs**
   - Periodically reassess KPIs to ensure they remain relevant as project goals evolve.
4. **Engage Stakeholders**
   - Share KPI performance with stakeholders to maintain alignment and accountability.

Real-World Applications

Example 1: Marketing Campaign

- **KPIs**: Click-through rates, cost per lead, social media engagement.
- **Tracking Method**: Combine data from marketing platforms into a Smartsheet KPI tracker.

Example 2: Software Development

- **KPIs**: Sprint velocity, defect density, release cycle time.
- **Visualization**: Use line charts to track sprint progress and cumulative defect counts.

Example 3: Event Planning

- **KPIs**: Registration numbers, vendor performance, attendee satisfaction.
- **Dashboard**: Embed widgets for real-time updates on ticket sales and feedback.

Troubleshooting Common Issues

1. Data Inconsistencies

- **Cause**: Incomplete or outdated data entries.
- **Solution**: Automate data collection and set reminders for updates.

2. Overwhelming Metrics

- **Cause**: Tracking too many metrics dilutes focus.
- **Solution**: Prioritize metrics that align with your objectives.

3. Poor Stakeholder Engagement

- **Cause**: Reports are overly technical or lack context.
- **Solution**: Simplify reports and highlight actionable insights.

Wrapping Up

Tracking KPIs and metrics in Smartsheet is crucial for monitoring progress, driving accountability, and achieving project success. By defining clear KPIs, setting up efficient tracking systems, and leveraging visual tools, you can keep stakeholders informed and your project on track.

Exporting and Sharing Reports

Exporting and sharing reports in Smartsheet ensures that your project insights are accessible to stakeholders, whether they use Smartsheet or not. This functionality allows you to provide updates in various formats, maintain data security, and customize how information is presented. In this chapter, we'll explore how to effectively export and share reports, enabling smooth collaboration and communication.

Why Export and Share Reports?

Key Benefits

1. **Accessible Insights**: Share project updates with stakeholders who may not have Smartsheet access.
2. **Customizable Formats**: Tailor reports for different audiences using formats like PDF or Excel.
3. **Streamlined Communication**: Deliver regular updates without manual effort through scheduled sharing.
4. **Improved Collaboration**: Enable seamless data sharing across teams and departments.

Exporting Reports

1. Export Formats

Smartsheet supports the following export formats:

- **PDF**: Ideal for static reports with a polished appearance.
- **Excel (XLSX)**: Suitable for detailed data analysis and further manipulation.
- **CSV**: Best for large datasets and integration with other tools.

2. Steps to Export

1. Open the report you want to export.
2. Click **File > Export As** and choose the desired format.
3. Adjust export settings (e.g., paper size for PDF, delimiter for CSV).
4. Click **Export** and save the file to your device.

3. Tips for Effective Exports

- **PDF Reports**: Use the print preview to adjust page settings for a clean layout.
- **Excel Exports**: Verify formulas and formatting transfer correctly.
- **CSV Files**: Double-check delimiters to ensure compatibility with external systems.

Sharing Reports

1. Real-Time Sharing in Smartsheet

Share reports directly with collaborators in Smartsheet:

1. Open the report and click **Share** in the toolbar.
2. Add the email addresses of the stakeholders you want to share with.
3. Set permissions:
   - **Viewer**: Stakeholders can view but not edit the report.

      ○ **Editor**: Stakeholders can view and make changes.
4. Click **Send** to notify collaborators.

2. Schedule Report Delivery

Automate regular updates by scheduling report deliveries:

1. Open the report and click **Automation > Schedule Report Delivery**.
2. Set the frequency (e.g., daily, weekly, or monthly).
3. Add recipients and customize the email message.
4. Save the schedule to automate future deliveries.

3. Public Links

For broader sharing, create a public link to the report:

1. Click **File > Publish Report**.
2. Enable the public link option and copy the URL.
3. Share the link with external stakeholders.
      ○ **Tip**: Use password protection for added security.

Enhancing Shared Reports

1. Add Visuals

- Include charts and graphs for stakeholders who prefer visual summaries.
- Ensure visuals are clear and aligned with the report's objectives.

2. Customize Views

- Tailor the report view based on stakeholder needs by applying filters or grouping data.
- Highlight key metrics or trends before sharing.

3. Embed Reports in Dashboards

- Combine reports with dashboards for an interactive, real-time overview.
- Use shortcut widgets to link to detailed reports.

Best Practices for Exporting and Sharing

1. **Understand Your Audience**
    ○ Choose the appropriate format and level of detail based on stakeholder preferences.
    ○ **Example**: Use PDFs for executives who need high-level insights, and Excel for analysts requiring granular data.
2. **Ensure Data Security**
    ○ Review permissions before sharing sensitive information.
    ○ Use password protection for shared links or exported files.
3. **Test Before Sending**
    ○ Review exported files for formatting issues or missing data.
4. **Standardize Report Schedules**
    ○ Establish a consistent schedule for delivering reports to maintain transparency and trust.

Real-World Applications

Example 1: Weekly Project Updates

- Export reports as PDFs and email them to stakeholders every Friday.
- Include a summary of key milestones and overdue tasks.

Example 2: Financial Analysis

- Share Excel exports of budget reports with the finance team for detailed analysis.
- Automate weekly updates to save time.

Example 3: Public Campaign Metrics

- Publish a public link to campaign performance reports for external partners.
- Use charts to showcase reach, engagement, and conversion rates.

Example 4: Cross-Team Collaboration

- Embed live reports in team dashboards for real-time access to shared data.

Troubleshooting Common Issues

1. Formatting Errors

- **Cause**: Mismatched column widths or unsupported formats during export.
- **Solution**: Adjust column sizes and verify settings before exporting.

2. Permission Issues

- **Cause**: Stakeholders unable to access shared reports.
- **Solution**: Confirm sharing permissions and ensure stakeholders have Smartsheet accounts if needed.

3. Outdated Data in Reports

- **Cause**: Data in the source sheet is not updated.
- **Solution**: Automate updates and ensure regular maintenance of source sheets.

Wrapping Up

Exporting and sharing reports in Smartsheet ensures seamless communication and collaboration across teams and stakeholders. By selecting the right format, scheduling automated updates, and maintaining data security, you can maximize the impact of your reports.

Section 7:
Integrations and Extensions

Connecting Smartsheet to Third-Party Tools

Integrating Smartsheet with third-party tools expands its capabilities, enabling seamless workflows, improved data sharing, and enhanced productivity. Whether you need to connect with project management software, communication platforms, or cloud storage, Smartsheet's integrations provide the flexibility to centralize your work and automate processes.

In this chapter, we'll explore the benefits of Smartsheet integrations, how to set them up, and examples of tools that work well with Smartsheet.

Why Integrate Smartsheet with Third-Party Tools?

Key Benefits

1. **Streamline Workflows**: Automate repetitive tasks and connect separate systems.
2. **Centralized Data**: Access all your project information in one platform.
3. **Improved Collaboration**: Sync communication tools and file-sharing platforms.
4. **Enhanced Reporting**: Pull data from various sources for comprehensive insights.
5. **Time Savings**: Reduce manual data entry and updates.

Setting Up Integrations

1. Using Smartsheet's App Marketplace

The Smartsheet App Marketplace offers pre-built integrations with popular tools.

1. Navigate to the **Smartsheet App Marketplace** from the Smartsheet interface.
2. Browse available integrations and select the tool you want to connect.
3. Follow the installation instructions, which may include logging into the third-party tool and granting permissions.

2. Leveraging Smartsheet API

For custom integrations, Smartsheet's API allows developers to build tailored solutions.

- Access API documentation at **developers.smartsheet.com**.
- Use APIs to automate workflows, update sheets, or retrieve data programmatically.

3. Using Automation Platforms

Platforms like Zapier, Make (formerly Integromat), and Power Automate enable easy connections between Smartsheet and other tools.

- **Example**: Automatically create a new row in Smartsheet when a form submission is received in Google Forms.

Common Integrations

1. Communication Tools

Microsoft Teams

- Sync Smartsheet updates with Teams channels to enhance collaboration.
- Use the Smartsheet for Teams integration to create, update, or share sheets directly within Teams.

Slack

- Receive real-time notifications in Slack for changes in Smartsheet.
- Automate reminders and alerts for upcoming deadlines.

2. File-Sharing Platforms

Google Drive

- Attach files stored in Google Drive to your Smartsheet rows.
- Save Smartsheet exports directly to your Drive.

Dropbox

- Link Dropbox files to tasks in Smartsheet for streamlined access.
- Share completed Smartsheet reports directly to a Dropbox folder.

3. Project Management Tools

Jira

- Sync tasks between Smartsheet and Jira to track development progress.
- Link Jira issues to Smartsheet rows for enhanced visibility.

Asana

- Map tasks in Smartsheet to projects in Asana for better alignment across teams.
- Import Asana data into Smartsheet for centralized reporting.

4. CRM Systems

Salesforce

- Create Smartsheet records from Salesforce opportunities or leads.
- Automate updates between Salesforce data and Smartsheet for real-time tracking.

HubSpot

- Sync marketing campaigns and contact data from HubSpot to Smartsheet.
- Use Smartsheet to manage HubSpot deal pipelines.

5. Cloud Storage and Productivity Tools

Microsoft OneDrive

- Attach files stored in OneDrive to Smartsheet rows.
- Save Smartsheet reports to OneDrive folders.

Office 365

- Create dynamic reports by linking Excel spreadsheets to Smartsheet.

- Automate task creation from Outlook emails.

Automating Workflows with Integrations

Example Workflows

1. **Task Management**:
   - Automatically create a Smartsheet task when a new issue is added in Jira.
   - Send notifications to Microsoft Teams when tasks are updated.
2. **Approval Processes**:
   - Use DocuSign integration to request and track approvals for contracts directly in Smartsheet.
3. **Data Consolidation**:
   - Pull marketing campaign data from HubSpot into Smartsheet to monitor performance.
4. **File Management**:
   - Sync files between Dropbox and Smartsheet for easy collaboration.

Best Practices for Smartsheet Integrations

1. **Identify Key Tools**
   - Focus on integrations that add the most value to your workflow.
2. **Start Simple**
   - Begin with pre-built integrations or automation platforms before diving into API-based custom solutions.
3. **Monitor and Maintain**
   - Regularly check integration settings to ensure they are functioning as intended.
4. **Train Your Team**
   - Provide training on how to use integrations effectively to maximize their benefits.
5. **Test Before Deploying**
   - Test integrations with a small dataset to verify accuracy and reliability.

Troubleshooting Integration Issues

Common Problems and Solutions

1. **Authentication Errors**
   - **Cause**: Incorrect login credentials or expired tokens.
   - **Solution**: Reauthorize the connection with updated credentials.
2. **Data Sync Failures**
   - **Cause**: Mismatched fields between Smartsheet and the third-party tool.
   - **Solution**: Verify field mappings and ensure data types are compatible.
3. **Integration Lag**
   - **Cause**: Large data sets or network issues.
   - **Solution**: Optimize data size and ensure a stable internet connection.

Real-World Applications

Example 1: Marketing Team Collaboration

- **Tools**: Smartsheet + Slack + Google Drive

- **Workflow**: Receive Slack notifications for task updates in Smartsheet. Attach campaign assets from Google Drive to Smartsheet tasks.

Example 2: Agile Development

- **Tools**: Smartsheet + Jira
- **Workflow**: Sync Jira issues with Smartsheet to track development progress alongside project timelines.

Example 3: Sales Pipeline Management

- **Tools**: Smartsheet + Salesforce
- **Workflow**: Import Salesforce leads into Smartsheet and use reports to track conversion rates.

Example 4: Event Planning

- **Tools**: Smartsheet + DocuSign + Dropbox
- **Workflow**: Track signed contracts in Smartsheet using DocuSign integration and store signed documents in Dropbox.

Wrapping Up

Connecting Smartsheet to third-party tools enhances its functionality, enabling seamless workflows and efficient collaboration. By leveraging integrations, you can centralize your project management efforts, reduce manual tasks, and ensure all team members and stakeholders are aligned.

Leveraging Smartsheet Labs for Innovation

Smartsheet Labs is an experimental platform that offers innovative tools and integrations to extend the functionality of Smartsheet. These tools, developed by Smartsheet or its community, are designed to solve specific problems, enhance workflows, and provide creative solutions for complex projects. While Smartsheet Labs tools are not officially supported, they can be valuable for exploring new possibilities and testing advanced capabilities.

What is Smartsheet Labs?

Key Features of Smartsheet Labs

1. **Experimental Tools**: Access cutting-edge tools that go beyond Smartsheet's core features.
2. **Free to Use**: Most tools in Smartsheet Labs are available for free.
3. **Community-Driven**: Includes tools developed by Smartsheet engineers and community contributors.

Caution with Labs Tools

- **Not Officially Supported**: Tools may have limited support or documentation.
- **Use at Your Own Risk**: Some tools may not work seamlessly with all workflows or versions of Smartsheet.

Accessing Smartsheet Labs

Steps to Access

1. Visit the [Smartsheet Labs website] (https://labs.smartsheet.com).
2. Browse the available tools and select one that fits your needs.
3. Follow the installation instructions, which may include logging into your Smartsheet account and granting permissions.

Popular Smartsheet Labs Tools

1. Calendar App

- **Description**: Visualize Smartsheet tasks and events in a calendar format.
- **Features**:
  - Sync Smartsheet rows with calendar events.
  - Filter by specific criteria (e.g., assigned team members or project phases).
- **Use Case**: Ideal for teams managing schedules or deadlines.

2. Pivot App

- **Description**: Create pivot tables from Smartsheet data.
- **Features**:
  - Summarize and group data by specific fields.
  - Generate reports with totals, averages, and other metrics.
- **Use Case**: Analyze resource allocation, budget summaries, or task distribution.

3. Data Uploader

- **Description**: Automate the import of data from external sources into Smartsheet.
- **Features**:
  - Map external data fields to Smartsheet columns.
  - Schedule recurring uploads for continuous updates.
- **Use Case**: Streamline the integration of data from CRMs or financial systems.

4. Map Chart

- **Description**: Create geographical visualizations using Smartsheet data.
- **Features**:
  - Plot data points on a map using location data.
  - Customize map styles and filters.
- **Use Case**: Track sales territories, event locations, or distribution points.

5. Org Chart Generator

- **Description**: Automatically generate organizational charts from Smartsheet data.
- **Features**:
  - Visualize hierarchical relationships.
  - Customize chart styles and levels.
- **Use Case**: Build team structures or project accountability charts.

Integrating Labs Tools with Your Workflow

1. Choose Tools that Solve Specific Problems

- Identify workflow challenges and select Labs tools designed to address those issues.
  - **Example**: Use the Calendar App to streamline task scheduling for a marketing campaign.

2. Combine Labs Tools with Core Smartsheet Features

- Leverage Labs tools to complement existing Smartsheet capabilities.
  - **Example**: Combine the Pivot App with Smartsheet dashboards to create detailed visualizations.

3. Automate Processes

- Use tools like the Data Uploader to automate data imports and reduce manual work.

Best Practices for Using Smartsheet Labs

1. **Test Before Implementing**
   - Experiment with tools in a controlled environment before applying them to critical projects.
2. **Monitor for Updates**
   - Regularly check the Smartsheet Labs website for new tools or updates to existing ones.
3. **Document Usage**
   - Keep a record of which Labs tools you use and how they integrate with your workflows.
4. **Engage the Community**
   - Share feedback and ideas in the Smartsheet community forums to improve existing tools or inspire new ones.

Real-World Applications

Example 1: Event Planning

- **Tools Used**: Calendar App, Map Chart
- **Workflow**:
  - Visualize event schedules with the Calendar App.
  - Use Map Chart to track event venues and attendee locations.

Example 2: Sales Performance Analysis

- **Tools Used**: Pivot App, Data Uploader
- **Workflow**:
  - Automate sales data imports with the Data Uploader.
  - Create pivot tables to analyze sales trends and team performance.

Example 3: Resource Allocation

- **Tools Used**: Pivot App, Org Chart Generator
- **Workflow**:
  - Use the Pivot App to summarize resource usage by department.
  - Generate an organizational chart to visualize team structures and responsibilities.

Troubleshooting Common Issues

1. Tool Compatibility Problems

- **Cause**: Labs tools may not support certain Smartsheet versions.
- **Solution**: Ensure your Smartsheet account is up to date and compatible with the tool.

2. Data Mapping Errors

- **Cause**: Incorrect mapping of Smartsheet data fields.
- **Solution**: Review field mappings and adjust configurations as needed.

3. Limited Support

- **Cause**: Labs tools are experimental and may not have comprehensive documentation.
- **Solution**: Seek help from Smartsheet community forums or experiment with alternative configurations.

Wrapping Up

Smartsheet Labs provides a playground for innovation, offering tools that push the boundaries of what you can achieve with Smartsheet. By exploring these experimental tools, you can enhance your workflows, discover new efficiencies, and stay ahead of the curve in project management.

Working with Mobile and Tablet Apps

The Smartsheet mobile and tablet apps enable you to stay connected and manage your projects from anywhere. Whether you're in a meeting, traveling, or working remotely, these apps provide access to your sheets, dashboards, and reports in a user-friendly interface optimized for smaller screens. This chapter explores how to make the most of Smartsheet's mobile and tablet apps, ensuring productivity on the go.

Why Use Smartsheet Mobile and Tablet Apps?

Key Benefits

1. **Anywhere Access**: Manage projects and collaborate with your team from any location.
2. **Real-Time Updates**: Receive notifications and stay updated on project progress.
3. **Ease of Use**: Simplified interface tailored for mobile devices.
4. **Enhanced Collaboration**: Quickly review tasks, comment on rows, and update statuses.

Setting Up the Smartsheet App

1. Download and Install

- **iOS**: Available on the App Store for iPhones and iPads.
- **Android**: Available on Google Play for smartphones and tablets.

2. Log In

- Use your Smartsheet credentials to access your account.
- Enable two-factor authentication (if applicable) for added security.

Navigating the Mobile Interface

1. Home Screen

- Displays recently accessed sheets, reports, and dashboards.
- Use the search bar to quickly find specific items.

2. Sheets and Reports

- Access your sheets and reports directly from the app.
- Use filters to view specific rows or apply sorting options.

3. Dashboards

- View interactive dashboards designed for mobile optimization.
- Drill down into widgets for detailed insights.

4. Notifications

- Access notifications to stay informed about updates, approvals, and comments.

Key Features of the Mobile App

1. Editing Sheets on Mobile

- Add, edit, or delete rows and columns.
- Update cell values, dropdown selections, or checkboxes.

2. Collaboration Tools

- Add comments directly to rows for contextual communication.
- Share sheets, reports, and dashboards via email or app links.

3. Task Management

- Mark tasks as complete, update statuses, or reassign ownership.
- Set reminders or update due dates with a few taps.

4. Photo and File Attachments

- Attach photos taken with your mobile device to rows.
- Upload files stored on your phone or cloud services like Google Drive.

5. Barcode Scanning

- Use the app's built-in barcode scanner to update inventory or assets directly in your sheet.

Using the App Offline

- Smartsheet's mobile app offers offline capabilities for viewing and editing sheets.
- Changes made offline will sync automatically when you reconnect to the internet.
- **Tip**: Download sheets or reports before going offline for uninterrupted access.

Optimizing for Tablets

1. Landscape Mode

- Tablets offer better visibility in landscape orientation.
- View dashboards and large datasets more effectively.

2. Split-Screen Functionality

- Use split-screen mode to work in Smartsheet while referencing another app, such as email or a browser.

Best Practices for Mobile and Tablet Use

1. **Customize Notifications**
   - Set preferences to receive only the most relevant alerts.
   - Avoid notification overload by focusing on critical updates.
2. **Optimize for Mobile Views**
   - Simplify sheet layouts by reducing unnecessary columns for easier mobile navigation.
3. **Leverage Templates**
   - Use pre-built templates for consistency and efficiency when creating sheets on mobile devices.

4. **Regular Syncing**
   - Ensure that offline changes are synced promptly to avoid data discrepancies.
5. **Train Your Team**
   - Educate your team on the app's features to maximize productivity and collaboration.

Real-World Applications

Example 1: Field Data Collection

- **Scenario**: A construction manager updates progress directly from the job site.
- **Workflow**:
  - Use the mobile app to upload photos of completed work and add notes for the team.

Example 2: Event Planning on the Go

- **Scenario**: An event coordinator tracks vendor deliverables while on-site.
- **Workflow**:
  - Update task statuses and collaborate with the team in real time.

Example 3: Sales Pipeline Updates

- **Scenario**: A sales representative updates lead statuses after client meetings.
- **Workflow**:
  - Use dropdowns and comments to log meeting outcomes and update the pipeline.

Troubleshooting Common Issues

1. Syncing Problems

- **Cause**: Poor internet connection.
- **Solution**: Check your connection or enable offline mode for temporary access.

2. App Crashes or Freezes

- **Cause**: Device performance issues or outdated app version.
- **Solution**: Restart the app or update it to the latest version.

3. Access Issues

- **Cause**: Incorrect permissions or account settings.
- **Solution**: Verify permissions in the desktop app or contact your administrator.

Wrapping Up

The Smartsheet mobile and tablet apps empower you to manage projects, collaborate with teams, and stay productive no matter where you are. By leveraging these tools effectively, you can ensure seamless workflows and maintain project momentum even on the go.

Exploring Marketplace Add-Ons

The Smartsheet Marketplace is a hub for add-ons and integrations designed to expand the platform's capabilities and streamline your workflows. These tools, developed by Smartsheet and its partners, help address specific business needs such as advanced analytics, workflow automation, and team collaboration. This chapter dives into the features of the Smartsheet Marketplace, popular add-ons, and how to integrate them into your workflows effectively.

What is the Smartsheet Marketplace?

The Smartsheet Marketplace is a collection of extensions and integrations that enhance the platform's functionality. These add-ons allow users to:

- Connect Smartsheet to other business tools.
- Automate processes and reduce manual work.
- Access specialized tools for reporting, data visualization, and collaboration.

Accessing the Marketplace

How to Find the Marketplace

1. Navigate to the **Apps and Integrations** section in your Smartsheet account.
2. Click on **Browse Apps** to explore available add-ons.
3. Visit the [Smartsheet Marketplace] (https://marketplace.smartsheet.com) directly for a full list of integrations.

Searching for Add-Ons

- Use keywords to search for specific functionalities.
- Filter results by category (e.g., collaboration, reporting, or automation).

Popular Add-Ons in the Marketplace

1. Smartsheet for Salesforce

- **Description**: Integrates Salesforce data with Smartsheet to manage customer relationships and sales pipelines.
- **Key Features**:
  - Sync Salesforce records with Smartsheet rows.
  - Automate updates between Salesforce and Smartsheet.
- **Use Case**: Perfect for sales teams tracking leads and opportunities.

2. Smartsheet for Jira

- **Description**: Connects Jira projects with Smartsheet to bridge project management and development workflows.
- **Key Features**:
  - Sync tasks, statuses, and priorities between Smartsheet and Jira.
  - Monitor development progress alongside project timelines.
- **Use Case**: Ideal for agile teams managing software development projects.

3. Microsoft 365 Integration

- **Description**: Seamlessly integrates Smartsheet with Microsoft tools like Outlook, Teams, and Excel.
- **Key Features**:
  - Convert emails into tasks or rows in Smartsheet.
  - Embed Smartsheet dashboards in Microsoft Teams.
- **Use Case**: Enhances collaboration for teams using Microsoft products.

4. Brandfolder

- **Description**: A digital asset management add-on that organizes and shares brand assets.
- **Key Features**:
  - Link Brandfolder assets directly to Smartsheet rows.
  - Automate asset updates across projects.
- **Use Case**: Useful for marketing teams managing large volumes of creative content.

5. Data Shuttle

- **Description**: Automates the import and export of data between Smartsheet and external systems.
- **Key Features**:
  - Schedule regular data uploads or downloads.
  - Map fields between Smartsheet and external data sources.
- **Use Case**: Perfect for teams managing dynamic data workflows.

Integrating Add-Ons with Smartsheet

Steps to Install Add-Ons

1. Visit the Smartsheet Marketplace and select an add-on.
2. Click **Install** and follow the on-screen instructions.
3. Grant permissions for the add-on to access your Smartsheet data.
4. Configure the integration by mapping fields or setting preferences.

Tips for Seamless Integration

- **Review Compatibility**: Ensure the add-on supports your Smartsheet version.
- **Test Before Full Deployment**: Pilot the add-on with a small dataset or team to identify potential issues.
- **Monitor Performance**: Evaluate the add-on's impact on workflow efficiency.

Advanced Use Cases

1. Automated Reporting

- **Add-Ons**: Data Shuttle, Power BI Integration
- **Workflow**: Automate the export of Smartsheet data into Power BI for advanced visualizations and reporting.

2. Marketing Campaign Management

- **Add-Ons**: Brandfolder, Smartsheet for Google Workspace
- **Workflow**: Link creative assets from Brandfolder to marketing project sheets and share campaign updates through Google Workspace.

3. IT Project Management

- **Add-Ons**: Smartsheet for Jira, Slack Integration
- **Workflow**: Sync development tasks in Jira with project timelines in Smartsheet, and notify teams of changes through Slack.

4. Resource Planning

- **Add-Ons**: Resource Management by Smartsheet
- **Workflow**: Use the Resource Management add-on to allocate and track team resources across multiple projects.

Best Practices for Using Marketplace Add-Ons

1. **Identify Your Needs**
   - Determine the specific gaps in your workflow that an add-on can address.
2. **Prioritize Essential Features**
   - Focus on add-ons with features that directly align with your team's goals.
3. **Maintain Data Security**
   - Review the privacy policy and security features of each add-on before installation.
4. **Provide Training**
   - Ensure team members are familiar with the new tools and how they integrate with Smartsheet.
5. **Monitor ROI**
   - Regularly assess the value an add-on provides by tracking improvements in efficiency or output.

Troubleshooting Common Issues

1. Integration Failure

- **Cause**: Incorrect setup or permissions.
- **Solution**: Revisit the installation process and confirm access permissions.

2. Performance Issues

- **Cause**: Add-on compatibility with your Smartsheet version.
- **Solution**: Check for updates or contact Smartsheet support for assistance.

3. Data Sync Errors

- **Cause**: Mismatched fields or unsupported data types.
- **Solution**: Verify field mappings and reconfigure as necessary.

Wrapping Up

Exploring the Smartsheet Marketplace is a great way to enhance your project management capabilities and address unique challenges. By integrating add-ons that align with your team's needs, you can automate processes, improve collaboration, and unlock new levels of productivity.

Section 8:
Project Planning Essentials

Defining Scope, Objectives, and Deliverables

Defining the scope, objectives, and deliverables is a foundational step in any successful project. It sets clear expectations, aligns stakeholders, and provides a roadmap for achieving desired outcomes. Smartsheet offers a range of tools to help project managers structure and manage these elements efficiently.

In this chapter, we'll explore how to define and document the scope, objectives, and deliverables using Smartsheet, and how to ensure alignment with your team and stakeholders.

Understanding Scope, Objectives, and Deliverables

1. Scope

The scope defines the boundaries of your project, outlining what will and will not be included.

- **Key Questions**:
    - What are the project's goals?
    - What resources are required?
    - What tasks and activities fall within the project's boundaries?

2. Objectives

Objectives are specific, measurable goals that the project aims to achieve.

- **SMART Framework**:
    - **Specific**: Clearly define what you want to achieve.
    - **Measurable**: Establish metrics to track progress.
    - **Achievable**: Ensure the goals are realistic given resources and constraints.
    - **Relevant**: Align objectives with broader organizational goals.
    - **Time-Bound**: Set deadlines for achieving each objective.

3. Deliverables

Deliverables are the tangible outputs or results produced during the project.

- **Examples**:
    - Reports, designs, or prototypes.
    - Completed tasks or milestones.
    - Final products or services ready for deployment.

Defining Scope in Smartsheet

1. Create a Scope Document

- Use a Smartsheet template for project scope or build a custom sheet.
- **Columns to Include**:
  - **Description**: Briefly define the scope element.
  - **Included**: List tasks, features, or activities within the scope.
  - **Excluded**: Clarify what is outside the scope.
  - **Owner**: Assign responsibility for scope elements.
  - **Status**: Track progress or approvals.

2. Visualize Scope with Hierarchies

- Use parent and child rows to organize scope details hierarchically.
  - **Example**: A parent row for "Website Redesign" with child rows for tasks like "UI Update" and "SEO Optimization."

3. Add Scope Validation

- Use comments or attachments to include approval notes or supporting documents.

Setting Objectives in Smartsheet

1. Use a Goals and Objectives Tracker

- Create a dedicated sheet to define and track objectives.
- **Columns to Include**:
  - **Objective Name**: Clearly label each objective.
  - **Description**: Provide details about the objective.
  - **Metrics**: Specify how success will be measured.
  - **Owner**: Assign accountability.
  - **Deadline**: Set target completion dates.
  - **Progress**: Use a dropdown or percentage column to track status.

2. Integrate Objectives into Dashboards

- Use widgets to display objectives, metrics, and progress visually.
- Highlight key milestones or deadlines to maintain focus.

3. Collaborate with Stakeholders

- Share the objectives sheet with stakeholders for input and alignment.
- Use real-time commenting to address questions or suggestions.

Documenting Deliverables in Smartsheet

1. Deliverables Tracker

- Use a sheet to document deliverables and their details.
- **Columns to Include**:
  - **Deliverable Name**: Provide a clear title.
  - **Description**: Detail the deliverable's purpose and requirements.
  - **Due Date**: Specify when the deliverable is expected.
  - **Dependencies**: Link deliverables to related tasks or milestones.
  - **Owner**: Assign accountability for completion.
  - **Status**: Track progress with dropdowns or checkboxes.

2. Use Attachments for Supporting Files

- Attach relevant files or documents to the deliverables row for easy access.
  - **Example**: Attach a prototype file or client approval email.

3. Track Deliverables Across Multiple Sheets

- Use cross-sheet linking to consolidate deliverables from various sheets into a central tracker.

Best Practices for Defining Scope, Objectives, and Deliverables

1. **Engage Stakeholders Early**
   - Collaborate with stakeholders during the planning phase to ensure alignment and avoid misunderstandings.
2. **Document Everything**
   - Maintain detailed records of scope, objectives, and deliverables in Smartsheet for transparency and accountability.
3. **Use Conditional Formatting**
   - Highlight overdue objectives or deliverables to prioritize actions.
4. **Review and Update Regularly**
   - Schedule periodic reviews to ensure scope, objectives, and deliverables remain relevant and achievable.
5. **Leverage Automation**
   - Set up automated reminders for deliverable deadlines or objective milestones.

Real-World Application

Example: Marketing Campaign

1. **Scope**: Define campaign goals, target audience, and excluded channels.
2. **Objectives**:
   - Increase website traffic by 25% in six months.
   - Generate 500 qualified leads by the end of the quarter.
3. **Deliverables**:
   - A complete campaign strategy document.
   - Five social media posts and two email newsletters.
   - Weekly performance reports.

Workflow in Smartsheet:

- Use a scope tracker to outline campaign boundaries.
- Set objectives in a goals tracker, with metrics linked to dashboards.
- Document deliverables in a dedicated sheet, attaching creative assets for collaboration.

Troubleshooting Common Challenges

1. Scope Creep

- **Cause**: Unplanned tasks or changes introduced mid-project.
- **Solution**: Use change request templates in Smartsheet to document and evaluate new requests.

2. Unclear Objectives

- **Cause**: Vague or unrealistic goals.
- **Solution**: Use the SMART framework to refine objectives.

3. Missed Deliverable Deadlines

- **Cause**: Poor time management or unclear dependencies.
- **Solution**: Use Gantt charts in Smartsheet to visualize timelines and dependencies.

Wrapping Up

Defining the scope, objectives, and deliverables is essential for successful project execution. Smartsheet provides a comprehensive platform to document, manage, and track these elements, ensuring alignment and accountability. By following the strategies in this chapter, you can set your projects up for success from the start.

Resource Allocation and Cost Considerations

Effective resource allocation and cost management are critical for project success. Inadequate planning can lead to resource shortages, overspending, or project delays. Smartsheet offers tools to help project managers allocate resources effectively and track costs to ensure projects stay on budget and on schedule.

In this chapter, we'll explore how to use Smartsheet to allocate resources, manage costs, and maintain financial oversight throughout the project lifecycle.

The Importance of Resource Allocation and Cost Management

Why Resource Allocation Matters

- **Efficiency**: Ensures that available resources are used optimally.
- **Avoid Overloading**: Prevents overburdening team members or exhausting physical resources.
- **Project Success**: Aligns resources with project priorities for timely delivery.

Why Cost Considerations Matter

- **Budget Compliance**: Helps avoid overspending.
- **Stakeholder Trust**: Provides transparency and accountability.
- **Profitability**: Ensures financial feasibility and return on investment (ROI).

Setting Up Resource Allocation in Smartsheet

1. Create a Resource Management Sheet

Use a dedicated Smartsheet to track resources.

- **Columns to Include**:
  - **Resource Name**: Name of the person, team, or asset.
  - **Role/Function**: Specify their role or purpose.
  - **Task Assigned**: Link to specific tasks or projects.
  - **Start Date/End Date**: Specify resource availability.
  - **Status**: Track resource utilization (e.g., available, in use, or unavailable).

2. Use Assignments in Task Sheets

- Assign resources directly to tasks in your project sheet.
- Add a **Resource Assigned** column to display the person or team responsible.

3. Leverage Resource Views

- Use Smartsheet's **Resource Management by Smartsheet** add-on to visualize resource allocation across projects.
- Identify over-allocated or underutilized resources in a centralized view.

Managing Costs in Smartsheet

1. Create a Budget Tracking Sheet

- Use Smartsheet to create a comprehensive budget tracker.
- **Columns to Include**:
  - **Expense Category**: Define cost categories (e.g., labor, materials, equipment).
  - **Budgeted Amount**: Specify the planned amount for each category.
  - **Actual Amount**: Record actual expenses.
  - **Variance**: Calculate the difference between budgeted and actual amounts.
  - **Approval Status**: Track whether expenses have been approved.

2. Track Costs Per Task

- Add cost-related columns to project sheets:
  - **Estimated Cost**: Initial cost projection.
  - **Actual Cost**: Costs incurred during task execution.
  - **Cost Variance**: Highlight differences to track overspending or savings.

3. Monitor Financial Metrics with Dashboards

- Build Smartsheet dashboards to visualize financial data.
  - Use widgets to display metrics like total budget, actual costs, and variance.
  - Add charts or graphs for a quick overview of financial health.

Optimizing Resource Allocation

1. Prioritize Tasks

- Use Smartsheet's **priority columns** to allocate resources to high-priority tasks first.
- Reallocate resources as priorities shift during the project.

2. Balance Workloads

- Use conditional formatting to highlight over-allocated resources.
- Adjust assignments to balance workloads and avoid burnout.

3. Track Resource Availability

- Use start and end date columns to monitor resource availability.
- Filter sheets to identify available resources for upcoming tasks.

Best Practices for Cost Management

1. Set a Contingency Budget

- Include a buffer in your budget to account for unexpected costs.
- Use Smartsheet formulas to calculate contingency amounts based on the total budget.

2. Monitor Expenses Regularly

- Schedule periodic reviews of actual costs versus the budget in Smartsheet.
- Use automated reminders to alert stakeholders about budget updates.

3. Document Cost Approvals

- Attach approval documents or comments to expense rows for transparency.

Real-World Applications

Example 1: Software Development Project

- **Resources**: Developers, designers, and testers.
- **Costs**: Labor, software licenses, and infrastructure.
- **Workflow in Smartsheet**:
    - Use resource views to balance workloads across development sprints.
    - Track licensing costs in a budget sheet with real-time variance calculations.

Example 2: Marketing Campaign

- **Resources**: Marketing team, freelance designers, and social media tools.
- **Costs**: Creative production, advertising spend, and event logistics.
- **Workflow in Smartsheet**:
    - Assign team members to campaign tasks and track hours worked.
    - Monitor advertising spend using a dashboard with key financial metrics.

Example 3: Construction Project

- **Resources**: Contractors, equipment, and materials.
- **Costs**: Labor, permits, and raw materials.
- **Workflow in Smartsheet**:
    - Use Gantt charts to schedule contractor work.
    - Record material costs and track against the allocated budget.

Troubleshooting Common Challenges

1. Over-Allocated Resources

- **Cause**: Assigning too many tasks to a single resource.
- **Solution**: Use Smartsheet's resource management features to reassign tasks and balance workloads.

2. Budget Overruns

- **Cause**: Inaccurate cost estimates or unexpected expenses.
- **Solution**: Monitor budget variance columns and adjust spending accordingly.

3. Resource Shortages

- **Cause**: Inadequate planning or unforeseen demands.
- **Solution**: Use Smartsheet's availability filters to identify backup resources.

Wrapping Up

Resource allocation and cost considerations are pivotal to project success. By leveraging Smartsheet's tools and features, you can plan resources effectively, manage costs efficiently, and keep your projects on track. Whether you're overseeing a small team or managing complex projects, these strategies ensure optimal use of resources and adherence to budgets.

Aligning Stakeholders and Teams

Aligning stakeholders and teams is critical to achieving project success. Clear communication, shared goals, and mutual understanding ensure that everyone is working toward the same objectives. Smartsheet provides a robust platform to facilitate this alignment by centralizing project information and fostering collaboration.

In this chapter, we'll explore strategies and Smartsheet tools for aligning stakeholders and teams effectively.

Importance of Stakeholder and Team Alignment

Why Stakeholder Alignment Matters

1. **Clarity**: Ensures stakeholders understand project goals and their role.
2. **Support**: Gains buy-in from key decision-makers.
3. **Conflict Prevention**: Reduces misunderstandings and conflicting priorities.

Why Team Alignment Matters

1. **Efficiency**: Keeps the team focused on prioritized tasks.
2. **Collaboration**: Promotes teamwork and accountability.
3. **Adaptability**: Enables quick responses to changes or challenges.

Setting Up Smartsheet for Stakeholder and Team Alignment

1. Centralized Project Hub

- Use Smartsheet as a single source of truth for project details.
- Create a dashboard to display:
    - Project objectives.
    - Key milestones.
    - Assigned tasks and progress updates.

2. Stakeholder Registry

- Maintain a stakeholder registry to identify key individuals and their roles.
- **Columns to Include**:
    - **Name**: Stakeholder's full name.
    - **Role**: Their position in the organization or project.
    - **Interest/Impact**: Level of interest and impact on the project.
    - **Communication Preferences**: Preferred frequency and method of updates.

Strategies for Aligning Stakeholders

1. Define Roles and Responsibilities

- Use a RACI (Responsible, Accountable, Consulted, Informed) matrix in Smartsheet.
- Clearly assign roles for each task or decision-making area.

2. Regular Updates and Reporting

- Schedule automated reports to keep stakeholders informed.
- Share interactive dashboards with live data for transparency.

3. Collaborative Input

- Use Smartsheet's commenting feature to gather stakeholder feedback directly within sheets.
- Attach documents or proposals for easy review and discussion.

Strategies for Aligning Teams

1. Shared Goals and Objectives

- Use Smartsheet to outline project objectives and share them with the team.
- Link objectives to specific tasks for clear alignment.

2. Task Assignments

- Assign tasks with clear deadlines and owners in Smartsheet project sheets.
- Use Gantt charts to visualize timelines and dependencies.

3. Real-Time Collaboration

- Encourage team collaboration using Smartsheet's comment and @mention features.
- Enable notifications to alert team members of updates or changes.

Tools for Alignment in Smartsheet

1. Dashboards

- Create dashboards for stakeholders and teams to provide real-time visibility into project progress.
- Include widgets for:
    - Task completion rates.
    - Budget tracking.
    - Upcoming milestones.

2. Automated Workflows

- Use automated workflows to notify stakeholders and team members of critical updates.
    - Example: Send reminders for overdue tasks or milestone approvals.

3. Sharing and Permissions

- Share sheets and dashboards with appropriate permissions.
    - Stakeholders: View-only access for progress updates.
    - Team Members: Edit access for task updates and collaboration.

Best Practices for Stakeholder and Team Alignment

1. **Engage Early**
    - Involve stakeholders and teams in the planning phase to gain their input and commitment.
2. **Communicate Regularly**
    - Schedule periodic check-ins to address concerns and align on priorities.

3. **Use Visual Tools**
   - Leverage Smartsheet's visual features, such as Gantt charts and dashboards, to make information easily digestible.
4. **Encourage Feedback**
   - Create a culture of open communication by encouraging feedback through comments and discussions in Smartsheet.
5. **Document Decisions**
   - Record key decisions and actions in Smartsheet to maintain a transparent record.

Real-World Applications

Example 1: Product Launch

- **Stakeholders**: Marketing, sales, and product development teams.
- **Workflow in Smartsheet**:
   - Use a dashboard to track the launch timeline and key deliverables.
   - Assign specific tasks to team members and share progress updates with stakeholders.

Example 2: Construction Project

- **Stakeholders**: Clients, contractors, and architects.
- **Workflow in Smartsheet**:
   - Maintain a stakeholder registry with communication preferences.
   - Use project sheets to track tasks and share updates with the team and stakeholders.

Example 3: Event Planning

- **Stakeholders**: Event coordinators, sponsors, and vendors.
- **Workflow in Smartsheet**:
   - Create a Gantt chart to visualize the event schedule.
   - Use automated reminders for vendor deadlines and approvals.

Troubleshooting Common Challenges

1. Conflicting Priorities

- **Cause**: Misaligned goals among stakeholders.
- **Solution**: Use a RACI matrix to clarify responsibilities and decision-making authority.

2. Communication Breakdowns

- **Cause**: Inconsistent updates or unclear messaging.
- **Solution**: Schedule automated updates and use Smartsheet comments for transparent communication.

3. Task Overlap

- **Cause**: Unclear task assignments.
- **Solution**: Assign specific owners to each task and track progress in Smartsheet.

Wrapping Up

Aligning stakeholders and teams is a cornerstone of successful project management. By leveraging Smartsheet's tools for collaboration, reporting, and task management, you can foster alignment, streamline communication, and drive project success.

Risk Management within Smartsheet

Managing risks effectively is essential for ensuring project success. Risks, if not identified and mitigated early, can derail progress, affect budgets, and compromise project goals. Smartsheet provides powerful tools for tracking, analyzing, and managing risks systematically, enabling project teams to stay proactive rather than reactive.

In this chapter, we'll explore how to leverage Smartsheet for risk management, including identifying potential risks, creating risk registers, assigning ownership, and monitoring mitigation efforts.

What is Risk Management?

Risk management involves identifying, assessing, and controlling potential events or situations that could negatively impact your project.

Types of Risks

1. **Financial Risks**: Budget overruns or unexpected costs.
2. **Operational Risks**: Delays in task completion or resource shortages.
3. **Strategic Risks**: Misalignment with organizational goals or stakeholder priorities.
4. **External Risks**: Market fluctuations, regulatory changes, or environmental factors.

The Risk Management Process

1. **Identify Risks**: Pinpoint potential issues that could arise.
2. **Assess Impact and Probability**: Evaluate how likely each risk is to occur and its potential impact.
3. **Develop Mitigation Strategies**: Plan actions to minimize risk impact.
4. **Monitor and Update**: Continuously track risks and adapt strategies as needed.

Setting Up Risk Management in Smartsheet

1. Create a Risk Register

A risk register is a centralized sheet where risks are documented and tracked.

- **Columns to Include**:
    - **Risk ID**: Unique identifier for each risk.
    - **Description**: Briefly describe the risk.
    - **Category**: Financial, operational, strategic, or external.
    - **Probability**: High, medium, or low likelihood.
    - **Impact**: High, medium, or low severity.
    - **Risk Score**: Multiply probability by impact to prioritize risks.
    - **Owner**: Assign responsibility for monitoring and mitigating the risk.
    - **Mitigation Plan**: Outline steps to address the risk.
    - **Status**: Open, closed, or in progress.

2. Use Conditional Formatting

- Highlight high-priority risks with red shading, medium risks with yellow, and low risks with green.
- Automatically update formatting based on risk scores.

3. Link Risks to Project Tasks

- Use cross-sheet linking to associate risks with specific tasks in your project plan.
- Example: Link a delay risk to a critical milestone in your timeline.

Monitoring Risks with Smartsheet Dashboards

1. Create a Risk Dashboard

- Use widgets to display:
    - Total number of risks.
    - Breakdown of risks by category.
    - Status of mitigation plans.
    - High-risk items requiring immediate attention.

2. Visualize Trends

- Use charts or graphs to track how risk levels change over time.
- Example: A bar chart showing the number of open risks each week.

3. Automate Alerts

- Set up automated reminders for risk owners to review and update risk statuses.
- Trigger alerts when high-priority risks are flagged or mitigation deadlines are approaching.

Best Practices for Risk Management in Smartsheet

1. **Engage Stakeholders Early**
    - Involve stakeholders in identifying risks to gain a comprehensive understanding of potential issues.
2. **Prioritize Proactively**
    - Focus on high-impact, high-probability risks first. Use Smartsheet formulas to calculate and sort risk scores.
3. **Document Everything**
    - Record all risks, even those deemed low priority, for reference and future analysis.
4. **Review Regularly**
    - Schedule periodic risk reviews to ensure mitigation plans remain effective and relevant.
5. **Leverage Collaboration Features**
    - Use comments and attachments to document discussions and actions related to each risk.

Real-World Applications

Example 1: Product Development

- **Risks**: Delays in component delivery, budget overruns, and design flaws.
- **Workflow in Smartsheet**:
    - Create a risk register to document potential delays and their mitigation plans.
    - Use dashboards to monitor critical risks and ensure alignment with stakeholders.

Example 2: Event Planning

- **Risks**: Weather disruptions, vendor cancellations, and attendee no-shows.
- **Workflow in Smartsheet**:

- Assign owners to each risk and track their mitigation efforts.
- Use automation to trigger updates on high-impact risks as the event date approaches.

Example 3: IT Infrastructure Upgrade

- **Risks**: Security breaches, system downtime, and budget overruns.
- **Workflow in Smartsheet**:
  - Link risks to specific project tasks, such as data migration or server installation.
  - Monitor risk statuses using a real-time dashboard shared with the IT team.

Troubleshooting Common Challenges

1. Underestimating Risks

- **Cause**: Inadequate initial assessment.
- **Solution**: Use stakeholder input and historical data to identify all potential risks comprehensively.

2. Delayed Mitigation Actions

- **Cause**: Lack of accountability.
- **Solution**: Assign clear ownership and set automated reminders in Smartsheet.

3. Risk Overload

- **Cause**: Tracking too many low-priority risks.
- **Solution**: Use conditional formatting to focus attention on high-priority items.

Wrapping Up

Effective risk management ensures that your project stays on track, even in the face of unexpected challenges. By leveraging Smartsheet to identify, assess, and mitigate risks, you can proactively address potential issues and maintain stakeholder confidence.

Section 9:
Effective Collaboration Strategies

Streamlining Communication Channels

Effective communication is the backbone of any successful project. Miscommunication or a lack of clarity can lead to delays, misunderstandings, and missed deadlines. Smartsheet provides powerful tools to centralize communication, reduce email overload, and ensure that project teams and stakeholders stay informed.

This chapter will guide you through strategies and best practices for using Smartsheet to streamline communication channels and enhance collaboration.

Importance of Streamlined Communication

Benefits of Centralized Communication

1. **Clarity**: Reduces the risk of misinterpretation by maintaining a single source of truth.
2. **Efficiency**: Eliminates time wasted searching for information in scattered emails or messages.
3. **Accountability**: Tracks conversations and decisions for future reference.

Common Communication Challenges

- **Information Silos**: Data scattered across tools and teams.
- **Overcommunication**: Excessive updates that dilute important information.
- **Delayed Responses**: Slow follow-ups due to unclear or inefficient channels.

Tools for Streamlined Communication in Smartsheet

1. Comments Feature

- Use comments to discuss specific tasks, rows, or issues directly in the context of the project sheet.
- @mention team members to notify them about updates or questions.
- Attach relevant files or images to comments for clarity.

2. Update Requests

- Automate update requests to gather information or status updates from team members.
- Schedule recurring requests for tasks that require regular check-ins.

3. Notifications and Alerts

- Set up automated alerts to inform team members about:
  - Task assignments or reassignments.
  - Changes to deadlines or dependencies.
  - Status updates for critical tasks.

4. Dashboards for Communication

- Create project dashboards to provide a centralized view of progress, upcoming deadlines, and key updates.
- Use widgets to display communication-related metrics, such as unresolved comments or pending approvals.

Best Practices for Streamlined Communication

1. Establish a Communication Plan

- Define the primary communication methods and channels within Smartsheet.
- Clearly state how and when team members should use comments, update requests, and notifications.

2. Use Consistent Naming Conventions

- Apply standard naming conventions for sheets, tasks, and comments to ensure clarity.
- Example: Use "Task - [Project Name] - [Priority Level]" for tasks.

3. Limit Email Overload

- Replace lengthy email chains with Smartsheet comments or update requests.
- Use email notifications only for critical updates that require immediate attention.

4. Encourage Real-Time Collaboration

- Leverage Smartsheet's real-time editing and commenting features to resolve issues on the spot.
- Use dashboards to host live project discussions with stakeholders.

Optimizing Communication Workflows

Workflow 1: Status Updates

- Use a project sheet with status columns (e.g., Not Started, In Progress, Completed).
- Automate reminders for team members to update task statuses weekly.
- Include a comments column for team members to provide context or raise concerns.

Workflow 2: Change Management

- Create a dedicated change log sheet to track and communicate project changes.
- Include columns for:
  - Change Description.
  - Impacted Tasks.
  - Requester.
  - Approval Status.
- Use automated notifications to alert stakeholders of significant changes.

Workflow 3: Meeting Summaries

- Use Smartsheet to document meeting notes and action items.
- Assign action items directly within the sheet and track progress.
- Share the sheet with attendees for transparency and accountability.

Real-World Applications

Example 1: Marketing Campaign

- **Challenge**: Coordinating communication across multiple teams.
- **Solution in Smartsheet**:
  - Use a shared campaign sheet with comments and update requests to centralize discussions.
  - Automate alerts for approaching deadlines to keep the team on track.

Example 2: Construction Project

- **Challenge**: Managing communication between contractors and clients.
- **Solution in Smartsheet**:
  - Create a dashboard displaying project milestones, progress updates, and client comments.
  - Use notifications to inform contractors about changes to schedules or tasks.

Example 3: IT Support Team

- **Challenge**: Tracking support tickets and updates.
- **Solution in Smartsheet**:
  - Use a ticketing sheet with a comments column for detailed issue discussions.
  - Set up automated notifications for priority ticket updates.

Troubleshooting Common Challenges

1. Missed Notifications

- **Cause**: Team members overlook automated alerts or emails.
- **Solution**: Encourage the use of Smartsheet's mobile app for real-time notifications.

2. Overcommunication

- **Cause**: Excessive updates dilute important information.
- **Solution**: Prioritize critical updates and use dashboards for non-urgent information.

3. Delayed Responses

- **Cause**: Lack of accountability or unclear communication workflows.
- **Solution**: Assign owners to tasks and use update requests to track responses.

Wrapping Up

Streamlining communication channels is essential for effective collaboration and project success. By leveraging Smartsheet's features, you can centralize communication, enhance transparency, and ensure that your team stays aligned.

Agile Project Management with Smartsheet

Agile project management is a flexible and iterative approach that emphasizes collaboration, adaptability, and customer-focused results. Originally developed for software development, Agile principles are now applied across industries to manage projects efficiently in dynamic environments. Smartsheet is an excellent tool for Agile teams, offering flexible and collaborative features to support iterative workflows, task prioritization, and continuous delivery.

This chapter will guide you through using Smartsheet for Agile project management, from setting up Agile workflows to tracking progress and facilitating collaboration.

Understanding Agile Project Management

Key Principles of Agile

1. **Customer Collaboration**: Prioritize customer involvement throughout the project.
2. **Responding to Change**: Adapt plans quickly based on feedback or shifting priorities.
3. **Iterative Development**: Break the project into smaller, manageable increments.
4. **Continuous Improvement**: Reflect and refine processes after each iteration.

Benefits of Agile in Smartsheet

- **Flexibility**: Easily adjust plans and priorities.
- **Transparency**: Centralized information ensures visibility for all stakeholders.
- **Collaboration**: Real-time updates and communication foster teamwork.

Setting Up Agile Workflows in Smartsheet

1. Create an Agile Backlog

- Use a sheet to capture and prioritize user stories or tasks.
- **Columns to Include**:
    - **Task/Story ID**: Unique identifier for each item.
    - **Description**: Brief details of the task or user story.
    - **Priority**: High, medium, or low.
    - **Sprint**: Assign to a specific sprint or iteration.
    - **Owner**: Responsible team member.
    - **Status**: To Do, In Progress, Done.

2. Visualize Workflow with Kanban Boards

- Use card view in Smartsheet to create a Kanban board.
- Organize cards by status (e.g., To Do, In Progress, Done) and drag them to reflect progress.

3. Plan Sprints

- Create a sprint planning sheet to manage tasks for each iteration.
- Assign tasks from the backlog to the current sprint based on team capacity and priority.
- Include start and end dates for the sprint.

Tracking Progress and Metrics

1. Use Dashboards for Real-Time Updates

- Create Agile dashboards to provide visibility into:
  - Sprint progress (tasks completed vs. remaining).
  - Burn-down charts to track work completion over time.
  - Team workload distribution.

2. Monitor Key Agile Metrics

- **Velocity**: Track the number of tasks or story points completed in each sprint.
- **Cycle Time**: Measure the time it takes to complete a task from start to finish.
- **Cumulative Flow**: Analyze the flow of tasks across different statuses to identify bottlenecks.

3. Automate Notifications

- Set up alerts to notify team members about task updates, due dates, or blockers.
- Use automated reminders to ensure tasks are completed on time.

Facilitating Collaboration

1. Daily Stand-Ups with Smartsheet

- Use a shared sheet to document daily updates:
  - **What was done yesterday?**
  - **What will be done today?**
  - **What are the blockers?**
- Share the sheet with the team and update it in real-time during stand-up meetings.

2. Centralized Communication

- Use comments to discuss specific tasks or blockers.
- Attach relevant documents, mockups, or feedback directly to tasks.

3. Stakeholder Involvement

- Share dashboards with stakeholders to keep them informed about progress and priorities.
- Use update requests to gather feedback on completed tasks or upcoming priorities.

Best Practices for Agile Project Management with Smartsheet

1. **Start Small**
   - Begin with a single sprint or project to refine your Smartsheet Agile workflow before scaling.
2. **Keep It Simple**
   - Avoid overcomplicating sheets or dashboards. Focus on essential information to maintain clarity.
3. **Prioritize Transparency**
   - Ensure all team members and stakeholders have access to relevant sheets and dashboards.
4. **Iterate and Improve**
   - Regularly review your Smartsheet Agile setup during sprint retrospectives. Identify areas for improvement.
5. **Celebrate Successes**
   - Use dashboards to showcase completed sprints and milestones, boosting team morale.

Real-World Applications

Example 1: Software Development

- **Workflow in Smartsheet**:
    - Use a Kanban board to manage feature development and bug fixes.
    - Track sprint velocity and adjust future sprint planning based on completed tasks.

Example 2: Marketing Campaigns

- **Workflow in Smartsheet**:
    - Manage campaign assets (e.g., copywriting, design, approvals) as user stories in a backlog.
    - Assign tasks to team members during sprint planning and track progress in card view.

Example 3: Product Launch

- **Workflow in Smartsheet**:
    - Create a backlog of launch activities (e.g., training, documentation, PR).
    - Use dashboards to monitor task completion and identify blockers.

Wrapping Up

Agile project management is a powerful approach for delivering high-quality results in dynamic environments. By leveraging Smartsheet's tools for backlog management, sprint planning, and collaboration, you can implement Agile workflows that drive success.

Remote and Distributed Teams Best Practices

With remote and distributed teams becoming the norm in today's work environment, effective collaboration across geographies and time zones is critical for project success. Smartsheet offers powerful tools to ensure seamless communication, coordination, and productivity among remote team members.

This chapter explores strategies and best practices for managing remote teams using Smartsheet, helping you leverage its features to overcome common challenges and maximize efficiency.

Challenges Faced by Remote and Distributed Teams

1. Communication Barriers

- Lack of face-to-face interaction can lead to misunderstandings.
- Important updates might get lost in lengthy email threads.

2. Coordination Difficulties

- Teams working across different time zones may face delays in decision-making.
- Tasks can fall through the cracks due to unclear responsibilities.

3. Maintaining Team Morale

- Remote work can lead to isolation and reduced team cohesion.

Best Practices for Managing Remote Teams with Smartsheet

1. Centralize Communication

- Use comments within Smartsheet to discuss tasks and projects.
- @mention team members to ensure they are notified of updates.
- Attach relevant documents directly to tasks to avoid scattered resources.

2. Enable Transparency with Dashboards

- Create dashboards to provide a real-time overview of project progress.
- Include widgets for task status, team workloads, and upcoming deadlines.
- Share dashboards with stakeholders and team members for consistent updates.

3. Leverage Automated Workflows

- Set up automated reminders for task deadlines, updates, and approvals.
- Use notification rules to alert team members of changes to shared sheets.

4. Facilitate Time Zone Coordination

- Include time zone details in task sheets to provide context for deadlines.
- Use conditional formatting to highlight tasks requiring urgent attention.
- Schedule recurring check-ins that accommodate multiple time zones.

5. Encourage Real-Time Collaboration

- Utilize Smartsheet's real-time editing features during virtual meetings.
- Assign action items immediately and track progress during discussions.

Smartsheet Features Tailored for Remote Teams

1. Card View for Visual Collaboration

- Use Card View to organize tasks visually, making workflows easier to understand.
- Drag and drop cards to update statuses in real-time.

2. Resource Management

- Use the Resource View to monitor team workloads and ensure equitable distribution of tasks.
- Adjust assignments dynamically to prevent burnout or underutilization.

3. Mobile App for On-the-Go Updates

- Ensure team members have access to the Smartsheet mobile app for real-time updates, regardless of their location.

Remote Team Collaboration Workflows

Workflow 1: Task Assignment and Tracking

1. Use a shared sheet to document tasks, owners, deadlines, and statuses.
2. Automate update requests for task progress to reduce follow-ups.
3. Track completion rates on a dashboard for visibility.

Workflow 2: Virtual Meeting Notes

1. Use Smartsheet to document meeting agendas and outcomes.
2. Assign action items with clear deadlines and responsible team members.
3. Share the sheet immediately after the meeting for alignment.

Workflow 3: Performance Reviews

1. Create a sheet to track key performance metrics for remote team members.
2. Schedule regular check-ins to discuss progress and gather feedback.
3. Use comments to document discussions and agreed-upon actions.

Enhancing Team Morale and Engagement

1. Celebrate Achievements

- Use dashboards to highlight team milestones and individual accomplishments.
- Include a "Kudos" section in sheets or dashboards for peer recognition.

2. Provide Training and Resources

- Use Smartsheet to share training materials, resources, and best practices.
- Track progress on training completion using automated reminders.

3. Host Virtual Team-Building Activities

- Create a shared sheet to gather ideas for virtual events or activities.
- Use comments to vote on and discuss event preferences.

Real-World Applications

Example 1: Global Marketing Team

- **Challenge**: Coordinating campaign efforts across continents.
- **Solution**:
  - Use dashboards to track campaign progress and metrics.
  - Set automated reminders for deliverable deadlines.

Example 2: IT Support Team

- **Challenge**: Providing consistent support across multiple time zones.
- **Solution**:
  - Use a ticketing sheet to log, assign, and track support issues.
  - Automate notifications for high-priority tickets to ensure quick responses.

Example 3: Software Development Team

- **Challenge**: Managing Agile workflows with distributed team members.
- **Solution**:
  - Use Smartsheet's Card View for Kanban-style task management.
  - Track sprint progress with dashboards and burn-down charts.

Troubleshooting Common Remote Team Challenges

1. Delayed Task Updates

- **Cause**: Team members forget to update task statuses.
- **Solution**: Automate update requests and reminders.

2. Information Overload

- **Cause**: Excessive notifications or overly detailed updates.
- **Solution**: Customize notification rules to focus on critical updates only.

3. Team Disengagement

- **Cause**: Lack of interaction or recognition.
- **Solution**: Regularly acknowledge team contributions and host virtual check-ins.

Wrapping Up

Managing remote and distributed teams requires intentional strategies and the right tools. Smartsheet provides a robust platform to streamline communication, enhance coordination, and maintain team engagement. By applying the practices outlined in this chapter, you can ensure that your remote team remains productive, collaborative, and aligned toward achieving project goals.

Reviewing and Approving Work Efficiently

Efficient review and approval processes are critical for project success, especially when managing complex workflows and collaborating with multiple stakeholders. Smartsheet provides powerful tools and features to streamline the review and approval process, ensuring that tasks are completed on time and meet quality standards.

This chapter explores best practices and workflows for setting up and managing review and approval processes within Smartsheet, helping you save time, reduce errors, and improve collaboration.

Importance of Streamlined Review and Approval

Key Benefits

1. **Time Savings**: Faster decision-making by eliminating delays.
2. **Transparency**: Clear visibility into the status of reviews and approvals.
3. **Accountability**: Clear assignment of responsibilities to stakeholders.
4. **Reduced Errors**: Prevent mistakes by establishing a formal approval process.

Setting Up Review and Approval Workflows in Smartsheet

1. Defining Roles and Responsibilities

Before creating workflows, identify the individuals or teams involved in the review and approval process:

- **Submitter**: The person who submits work for review.
- **Reviewer**: The individual responsible for providing feedback.
- **Approver**: The decision-maker who gives the final approval.

2. Structuring Your Sheet

Design a Smartsheet with the following key columns:

- **Task Name**: Describes the item to be reviewed.
- **Assigned To**: Specifies the person responsible for review or approval.
- **Status**: Tracks whether the task is "Pending Review," "Approved," or "Rejected."
- **Comments/Feedback**: A column for reviewers to provide notes or suggestions.
- **Due Date**: Ensures timely completion of reviews.

3. Automating Approval Requests

Use automated workflows to streamline the review process:

- Set up an **Update Request** to notify reviewers when work is ready for review.
- Create an **Approval Request** automation to notify approvers when a task requires their attention.
- Send reminders for overdue tasks to keep the process on track.

Key Features in Smartsheet for Reviews and Approvals

1. Approval Request Automation

Smartsheet allows you to set up automated workflows for approvals:

- Automatically notify the approver when a task is marked as "Ready for Approval."
- Use conditional logic to route tasks to different approvers based on criteria (e.g., department, priority).

2. Comments and Attachments

- Use the **Comments** section for reviewers to provide feedback directly on the task.
- Attach files or screenshots for detailed explanations or annotations.

3. Row-Level Permissions

- Restrict editing rights to specific users to ensure only authorized individuals can make changes.
- Allow reviewers to edit only their assigned rows while keeping the rest of the sheet protected.

4. Activity Log

- Use the Activity Log to track who made changes, when they occurred, and what was updated.
- Ensure accountability and transparency throughout the review process.

Workflow Example: Review and Approval Process

Step-by-Step Guide

1. **Submission**: The submitter updates the sheet, marking the task as "Ready for Review."
2. **Notification**: An automated workflow sends a notification to the assigned reviewer.
3. **Review**: The reviewer updates the **Comments** column with feedback and changes the status to "Reviewed."
4. **Approval**:
   - If approved, the approver changes the status to "Approved."
   - If rejected, the approver updates the **Comments** column with the reason for rejection and reassigns the task to the submitter.
5. **Completion**: The submitter addresses the feedback and resubmits for review.

Best Practices for Efficient Reviews

1. Use Dashboards for Visibility

- Create a dashboard to track the status of all tasks requiring review or approval.
- Include widgets for "Pending Reviews," "Overdue Approvals," and "Recently Approved Tasks."

2. Set Clear Deadlines

- Use the **Due Date** column to specify deadlines for reviews and approvals.
- Automate reminders to ensure stakeholders complete their tasks on time.

3. Standardize Feedback

- Provide guidelines for reviewers on how to document feedback.
- Use dropdown lists for common review outcomes, such as "Needs Revision" or "Approved with Minor Edits."

4. Monitor Performance

- Use reports to analyze the efficiency of your review process.
- Identify bottlenecks by tracking how long tasks remain in the "Pending Review" or "Pending Approval" stage.

Real-World Applications

Example 1: Marketing Campaign Approval

- **Scenario**: A marketing team needs to approve creative assets before launching a campaign.
- **Solution**:
  - Use Smartsheet to assign reviews to stakeholders from design, legal, and management.
  - Automate approval workflows to ensure timely sign-off.

Example 2: Software Feature Review

- **Scenario**: An IT team needs to review and approve new feature requests.
- **Solution**:
  - Use conditional logic to route approvals based on project size or priority.
  - Track feedback and revisions in the comments section for transparency.

Example 3: Event Planning Coordination

- **Scenario**: An events team requires approval on budgets, venue choices, and vendor contracts.
- **Solution**:
  - Attach vendor proposals directly to the sheet for review.
  - Use automated workflows to notify decision-makers of pending approvals.

Troubleshooting Common Issues

1. Delays in Approvals

- **Cause**: Stakeholders forget to respond to approval requests.
- **Solution**: Use automated reminders and escalation workflows to notify alternate approvers.

2. Incomplete Feedback

- **Cause**: Reviewers provide vague or insufficient comments.
- **Solution**: Include a **Feedback Template** in the sheet to guide reviewers.

3. Overlapping Responsibilities

- **Cause**: Multiple stakeholders are unclear on who is responsible for approval.
- **Solution**: Clearly define roles in the sheet and assign tasks to specific individuals.

Wrapping Up

Streamlining your review and approval processes with Smartsheet ensures timely decision-making, improves accountability, and fosters effective collaboration among stakeholders. By leveraging Smartsheet's automation features, dashboards, and reporting tools, you can eliminate bottlenecks and keep your projects on track.

Section 10:
Advanced Workflows and Automations

Approval Processes and Automated Actions

Efficient approval processes are essential for managing projects, ensuring compliance, and maintaining accountability. Smartsheet provides powerful tools for automating approvals and streamlining workflows. By leveraging Smartsheet's automation capabilities, teams can eliminate delays, reduce manual work, and improve transparency in their approval workflows.

This chapter focuses on setting up approval processes, using automation to manage actions, and best practices for optimizing these workflows.

The Importance of Approval Processes

Approval processes are critical for:

- **Maintaining Quality**: Ensuring work meets required standards before moving to the next phase.
- **Accountability**: Clearly defining who is responsible for approvals.
- **Efficiency**: Reducing bottlenecks by automating repetitive tasks.
- **Compliance**: Keeping an audit trail of all approvals for regulatory or organizational requirements.

Setting Up Approval Workflows

1. Identifying Approval Points

Determine where approvals are necessary within your workflow. Common approval points include:

- Budget or resource allocation.
- Task or project completion.
- Document or deliverable submission.

2. Structuring Your Sheet for Approvals

Include columns in your sheet to track approvals effectively:

- **Approval Status**: A dropdown column with options like "Pending," "Approved," and "Rejected."
- **Approver**: Specifies the individual or team responsible for approval.
- **Comments**: Provides space for approvers to leave feedback or notes.
- **Due Date**: Ensures timely responses to approval requests.

Automating Approval Requests

Smartsheet's **Automation Workflows** allow you to create rules that trigger approval requests. Follow these steps to set up automated approvals:

Step 1: Create a Trigger

- Define when the approval process should begin.
- Example: A new row is added, or the status is changed to "Ready for Approval."

Step 2: Add an Action

- Set the action to **Request an Approval**.
- Specify the approver(s) by selecting a column or entering specific email addresses.

Step 3: Customize the Message

- Include relevant details in the notification, such as the task name, due date, and any attached files.

Step 4: Add Conditions

- Use conditions to route approvals dynamically based on criteria like project type or priority.

Step 5: Define Follow-Up Actions

- Automate actions based on the approval outcome:
  - **If Approved**: Mark the task as "Approved" and notify relevant team members.
  - **If Rejected**: Update the status to "Rejected" and notify the submitter with comments.

Advanced Approval Scenarios

Multi-Level Approvals

For workflows requiring multiple levels of approval:

- Create sequential workflows that send the task to the next approver after the previous one has approved.
- Example: A marketing budget approval may require team leader approval followed by department head approval.

Parallel Approvals

For tasks requiring input from multiple stakeholders simultaneously:

- Send approval requests to all approvers at the same time.
- Use automation to mark the task as "Approved" only when all responses are affirmative.

Conditional Approvals

Route approval requests dynamically:

- Example: Tasks with a budget over $10,000 are routed to a finance approver, while others go to a project manager.

Managing Automated Actions

Common Automated Actions in Approval Workflows

1. **Notifications**: Keep team members informed about approval status changes.
2. **Updates**: Automatically update columns based on approval outcomes.

3. **Reminders**: Send reminders to approvers for pending requests.

Example Automation Workflow

1. **Trigger**: When a task is marked as "Ready for Approval."
2. **Condition**: If the task priority is "High."
3. **Action**: Send an approval request to the project manager.
4. **Follow-Up**:
   - If approved, update the status to "Approved" and notify the submitter.
   - If rejected, update the status to "Rejected" and return the task to the submitter with comments.

Best Practices for Approval Processes

1. Define Clear Roles

- Assign specific approvers to avoid confusion and delays.
- Use the **Assigned To** column to clearly define responsibilities.

2. Set Deadlines

- Use the **Due Date** column to ensure timely approvals.
- Automate reminders to follow up on overdue tasks.

3. Maintain Transparency

- Share the approval workflow with all stakeholders.
- Use Smartsheet dashboards to provide visibility into the status of approvals.

4. Audit Approval History

- Use the Activity Log to track who approved or rejected tasks and when.
- Export approval logs for compliance or reporting purposes.

Troubleshooting Common Challenges

1. Delayed Approvals

- **Cause**: Approvers forget to respond to requests.
- **Solution**: Use automated reminders and escalation workflows.

2. Misrouted Requests

- **Cause**: Approval requests are sent to the wrong person.
- **Solution**: Double-check automation conditions and approver assignments.

3. Incomplete Feedback

- **Cause**: Approvers provide vague or insufficient comments.
- **Solution**: Encourage approvers to use the **Comments** column for detailed feedback.

Real-World Application

Example: Marketing Campaign Approval Workflow

- **Scenario**: A marketing team needs approval for a new campaign.
- **Process**:
  - Submit campaign details in Smartsheet.
  - Automatically route the request to the creative director for initial review.
  - If approved, send it to the marketing manager for final approval.
  - Notify the submitter of the final decision and next steps.

Example: Vendor Contract Approval

- **Scenario**: The procurement team needs to approve vendor contracts.
- **Process**:
  - Submit contract details and attach relevant documents.
  - Trigger a multi-level approval workflow involving the legal team and finance department.
  - Automatically log approvals in Smartsheet for compliance purposes.

Wrapping Up

Smartsheet's approval processes and automation features simplify complex workflows, improve collaboration, and reduce delays. By leveraging these tools effectively, you can enhance project efficiency, ensure accountability, and meet critical deadlines.

Building Complex Formulas and Logic

Smartsheet's formula capabilities empower users to perform advanced calculations, streamline decision-making, and optimize workflows. By understanding and applying complex formulas and logic, you can automate processes, generate dynamic insights, and improve data accuracy. This chapter dives into creating and using advanced formulas, combining them with logical operations, and exploring real-world applications.

The Role of Complex Formulas in Smartsheet

Advanced formulas and logic allow you to:

- **Automate Processes**: Eliminate manual calculations by automating data processing.
- **Generate Insights**: Create metrics, KPIs, and dashboards for better decision-making.
- **Improve Accuracy**: Reduce errors in repetitive or complex calculations.
- **Enhance Reporting**: Transform raw data into actionable insights.

Key Formula Types

1. Logical Formulas

Logical functions like IF, AND, and OR help create conditions within your formulas.

- **Example**:

    ```
    =IF([Task Status]@row = "Complete", "Approved", "Pending")
    ```

    - If the task status is "Complete," mark the row as "Approved." Otherwise, mark it as "Pending."

2. Date and Time Functions

Date-related formulas are essential for tracking deadlines and durations.

- **Example**:

    ```
    =TODAY() - [Start Date]@row
    ```

    - Calculates the number of days since the start date.

3. Lookup Functions

Use functions like VLOOKUP and INDEX(MATCH) to reference data across sheets.

- **Example**:

    ```
    =INDEX({Sheet Range}, MATCH([ID]@row, {ID Range}, 0))
    ```

    - Finds a value in a range based on a matching ID.

4. Aggregates and Summaries

Functions like SUMIF and COUNTIF help summarize data based on conditions.

- **Example**:

```
=SUMIF([Project]@row:[Project]@row, "Marketing",
[Budget]@row:[Budget]@row)
```

  - Totals the budget for marketing-related projects.

Combining Logical Operations

Nested IF Statements

Create complex conditions using nested IF formulas.

- **Example**:

```
=IF([Status]@row = "Complete", "Approved", IF([Status]@row = "In
Progress", "Pending", "Rejected"))
```

  - Outputs "Approved" if the status is "Complete," "Pending" if "In Progress," or "Rejected" otherwise.

Using AND/OR for Multi-Condition Logic

Combine multiple conditions in one formula.

- **Example**:

```
=IF(AND([Priority]@row = "High", [Due Date]@row < TODAY()), "Overdue",
"On Track")
```

  - Marks tasks as "Overdue" if priority is high and the due date has passed.

Advanced Formula Techniques

Cross-Sheet Formulas

Reference data from another sheet to build interconnected workflows.

- **Example**:

```
=VLOOKUP([Project ID]@row, {Project Details Sheet}, 2, false)
```

  - Retrieves project details from a linked sheet.

Conditional Rollups

Use formulas like COUNTIF or SUMIF to create conditional summaries.

- **Example**:

```
=COUNTIF([Status]:[Status], "Complete")
```

  - Counts the number of completed tasks.

Error Handling

Incorporate IFERROR to manage formula errors.

- **Example**:

```
=IFERROR(VLOOKUP([Key]@row, {Reference Data}, 2, false), "Not Found")
```

   - Outputs "Not Found" if the lookup value is missing.

Automating Decisions with Formulas

Triggering Alerts or Updates

- Use formulas to update fields dynamically, triggering alerts or workflow actions.
- **Example**: Set a "Flag" column to mark overdue tasks:

```
=IF([Due Date]@row < TODAY(), "▲", "")
```

Prioritization Systems

- Combine conditions to assign priorities automatically.
- **Example**:

```
=IF([Urgency]@row = "High", "1", IF([Urgency]@row = "Medium", "2", "3"))
```

   - Ranks tasks by urgency level.

Real-World Applications

Budget Tracking

- Use formulas to track expenses and identify over-budget items.
- **Example**:

```
=IF([Spent Amount]@row > [Budget Amount]@row, "Over Budget", "Within Budget")
```

Project Progress Dashboards

- Summarize project completion percentages.
- **Example**:

```
=SUMIF([Status]:[Status], "Complete", [Duration]:[Duration]) /
SUM([Duration]:[Duration]) * 100
```

   - Calculates the percentage of completed project tasks.

Resource Management

- Track team availability with conditional formulas.
- **Example**:

```
=IF([Hours Logged]@row > [Available Hours]@row, "Overutilized",
"Available")
```

Best Practices for Complex Formulas

1. **Use Descriptive Column Names**
   - Clear names make formulas easier to understand and maintain.
2. **Test Formulas Incrementally**
   - Break down complex formulas into smaller parts for testing.
3. **Document Your Formulas**
   - Include notes explaining formula logic for future reference.
4. **Optimize for Performance**
   - Minimize unnecessary calculations, especially for large sheets.
5. **Leverage Cross-Sheet References Wisely**
   - Use linked sheets for data integrity and avoid duplicating information.

Troubleshooting Common Issues

Issue 1: Formula Errors

- **Cause**: Incorrect syntax or references.
- **Solution**: Check for missing parentheses or typos.

Issue 2: Performance Issues

- **Cause**: Large datasets or complex formulas.
- **Solution**: Use summary sheets or dashboards to simplify calculations.

Issue 3: Unexpected Results

- **Cause**: Data inconsistencies.
- **Solution**: Validate input data and check for hidden characters.

Wrapping Up

Building complex formulas and logic in Smartsheet is a powerful way to enhance workflows, streamline processes, and unlock actionable insights. With a solid understanding of advanced functions and their applications, you can drive efficiency, accuracy, and collaboration in your projects.

Integrating Forms for Data Collection

Forms are a powerful feature in Smartsheet that simplify data collection and improve the accuracy of project information. By integrating forms into your workflows, you can gather input from team members, stakeholders, or external parties efficiently. This chapter will guide you through creating and customizing forms, automating their workflows, and leveraging them for data-driven decision-making.

Why Use Smartsheet Forms for Data Collection?

Smartsheet forms are designed to:

- **Streamline Data Input**: Collect information directly into your sheets without manual data entry.
- **Ensure Consistency**: Standardize data collection across multiple contributors.
- **Enhance Collaboration**: Share forms with both internal and external users.
- **Improve Accessibility**: Enable data collection from any device, anywhere.
- **Automate Workflows**: Trigger actions based on form submissions.

Creating a Form

Step 1: Open the Form Builder

1. Navigate to the sheet where you want to collect data.
2. Click on the **Forms** dropdown in the toolbar.
3. Select **Create Form** to launch the form builder interface.

Step 2: Add Fields to the Form

- Smartsheet automatically adds fields based on your sheet's columns.
- **Customizing Fields**:
  - Rename labels for clarity.
  - Add placeholder text for guidance.
  - Make fields required to ensure necessary data is collected.

Step 3: Customize the Form Layout

- **Reorder Fields**: Drag and drop fields to set the desired order.
- **Add Sections**: Group related fields under headers for better organization.
- **Enable Logic**: Use conditional logic to show or hide fields based on responses.

Step 4: Style the Form

- Apply branding elements such as your company logo and colors.
- Add a description or instructions at the top of the form for context.

Sharing Your Form

Form Link

- Generate a public or private link to share the form.
- **Best Practices**:
  - Use a URL shortener for easier sharing.

    ○ Include the link in emails, websites, or project communications.

Embedding Forms

- Embed forms in websites or intranet pages for direct access.

QR Codes

- Generate QR codes linked to your form, allowing users to scan and submit data via mobile devices.

Automating Workflows with Forms

Notifications on Submission

Set up alerts to notify team members whenever a new form is submitted.

- Navigate to **Automation** > **Create Workflow**.
- Configure triggers for new rows added by form submissions.

Approval Processes

Route form submissions through approval workflows.

- **Example**: When a request is submitted, send it to the manager for approval before adding it to the project pipeline.

Data Validation

Use conditional formatting or formulas to validate form-submitted data automatically.

- **Example**: Flag entries where budgets exceed predefined limits.

Best Practices for Form Design

1. **Simplify the Layout**
   - Use concise labels and avoid overloading forms with too many fields.
2. **Enable Conditional Logic**
   - Tailor the form experience by displaying only relevant questions.
3. **Test Before Sharing**
   - Submit test entries to ensure the form behaves as expected.
4. **Secure Access**
   - Protect sensitive data by restricting form access with Smartsheet's sharing settings.
5. **Regularly Review Submissions**
   - Periodically check for accuracy and completeness of form entries.

Real-World Applications

Example 1: Employee Onboarding

- Collect employee information, assign training tasks, and track onboarding progress through automated workflows triggered by form submissions.

Example 2: Event Registrations

- Use forms to manage attendee sign-ups, dietary preferences, and session selections.

Example 3: Customer Feedback

- Distribute forms for post-project reviews and collect actionable insights to improve services.

Troubleshooting Common Issues

Problem: Missing Data in Submissions

- **Cause**: Fields not marked as required.
- **Solution**: Update the form to make key fields mandatory.

Problem: Users Unable to Access the Form

- **Cause**: Restricted sharing settings.
- **Solution**: Review and adjust the form's sharing permissions.

Problem: Duplicate Submissions

- **Cause**: Users submitting the form multiple times.
- **Solution**: Add a note to the form confirming that submissions were received.

Leveraging Forms for Long-Term Success

Integrating forms into your Smartsheet workflows is a game-changer for streamlining data collection. Whether you're managing internal operations or engaging with external stakeholders, forms provide a seamless way to gather, validate, and act on critical information.

Optimizing Workflows with Conditional Paths

Conditional paths in Smartsheet allow you to create advanced workflows that adapt based on specific triggers, conditions, and actions. This functionality empowers teams to manage complex processes, automate repetitive tasks, and ensure seamless project execution. In this chapter, we'll explore how to design and implement conditional workflows that drive efficiency and improve project outcomes.

Understanding Conditional Paths

A **conditional path** is a workflow feature that allows Smartsheet to perform different actions depending on predefined conditions. This is particularly useful for:

- Managing approval processes.
- Routing tasks to the correct team or individual.
- Automating responses based on project status or other criteria.

Key Benefits

- **Customization**: Tailor workflows to meet specific project needs.
- **Efficiency**: Eliminate manual intervention in routine tasks.
- **Accuracy**: Reduce the risk of errors by automating decision-making.

Creating a Conditional Workflow

Step 1: Access the Workflow Builder

1. Open the sheet where you want to implement the workflow.
2. Go to **Automation** in the toolbar.
3. Select **Create a Workflow** to launch the builder.

Step 2: Define the Trigger

Triggers are the events that initiate the workflow. Examples include:

- **When rows are added or changed**: Useful for updates to task status or priority.
- **When a date is reached**: Ideal for sending reminders or escalating delays.
- **When comments are added**: Helps in tracking discussions and decisions.

Step 3: Add Conditions

Conditions determine the workflow's behavior. For example:

- **Task Priority**: Apply specific actions for "High Priority" tasks.
- **Approval Status**: Route requests differently based on whether they're approved or rejected.
- **Custom Fields**: Use any column in the sheet to set conditions, such as department, budget, or deadline.

Step 4: Define Actions

Actions are the tasks Smartsheet performs when conditions are met. Examples include:

- **Alerts**: Notify team members of changes or updates.
- **Record Updates**: Automatically update specific columns based on triggers.

- **Approvals**: Request, track, and record approvals in the sheet.

Example: Multi-Step Approval Workflow

Scenario

You're managing a project where budget approvals depend on the request amount:

- **Less than $5,000**: Approved by the project manager.
- **5,000 - 10,000**: Requires finance team approval.
- **More than $10,000**: Escalated to the executive team.

Steps to Create

1. **Trigger**: When a new request is submitted via a form or added to the sheet.
2. **Condition**:
   - If **Amount < $5,000**, assign approval to the project manager.
   - If **Amount ≥ 5,000 and ≤ 10,000**, assign approval to the finance team.
   - If **Amount > $10,000**, notify the executive team.
3. **Actions**:
   - Send alerts to the appropriate approvers.
   - Update the "Approval Status" column with "Pending," "Approved," or "Rejected."

Best Practices for Conditional Workflows

1. **Start Simple**
   Begin with basic workflows and gradually add complexity as needed.
2. **Use Clear Labels**
   Name conditions and actions descriptively to make workflows easy to understand and maintain.
3. **Test Thoroughly**
   Test workflows in a controlled environment before deploying them widely.
4. **Leverage Alerts**
   Use alerts to keep team members informed of changes and decisions in real-time.
5. **Review and Optimize**
   Regularly review workflows to ensure they align with evolving project needs.

Common Use Cases

Task Assignment

- Route tasks automatically to team members based on expertise or workload.

Client Requests

- Send different notifications or responses based on the type of request submitted.

Escalation Processes

- Ensure timely resolution by escalating overdue tasks to senior management.

Budget Tracking

- Trigger actions based on budget thresholds to ensure financial control.

Troubleshooting Workflow Issues

Problem: Workflow Not Triggering

- **Cause**: Trigger conditions not met.
- **Solution**: Double-check trigger settings and test with sample data.

Problem: Incorrect Actions Performed

- **Cause**: Misconfigured conditions or actions.
- **Solution**: Review and edit the workflow logic.

Problem: Workflow Overlaps

- **Cause**: Multiple workflows affecting the same rows.
- **Solution**: Consolidate workflows or set execution priorities.

Maximizing Workflow Potential

Conditional paths are a versatile tool that can transform how teams manage their projects in Smartsheet. By leveraging these workflows, you can create systems that adapt dynamically to changing project requirements, reducing manual intervention and improving overall efficiency.

Section 11:
Best Practices and Troubleshooting

Standardizing Templates and Processes

Standardization is a cornerstone of successful project management. In Smartsheet, standardizing templates and processes ensures consistency, improves collaboration, and enhances efficiency across teams and projects. This chapter explores how to create and implement standardized templates and processes in Smartsheet to drive predictable and repeatable success.

Why Standardization Matters

Key Benefits

- **Consistency Across Projects**: Maintain a uniform structure and style for all projects, ensuring a professional and organized approach.
- **Improved Efficiency**: Save time by eliminating the need to recreate layouts or workflows for every new project.
- **Error Reduction**: Minimize errors by standardizing formulas, workflows, and data structures.
- **Streamlined Collaboration**: Foster better communication by ensuring all team members work with familiar templates.

Creating Standardized Templates

Smartsheet allows you to save custom templates tailored to your organizational needs.

Step 1: Design a Master Sheet

1. **Define the Purpose**: Identify the project type or process the template will support (e.g., project tracking, task management, resource allocation).
2. **Include Essential Elements**: Ensure your template contains all necessary columns, rows, formulas, and workflows. Examples include:
   - Task Name
   - Start and End Dates
   - Assigned To
   - Status
   - Dependencies
3. **Add Conditional Formatting**: Highlight critical elements such as overdue tasks, high-priority items, or tasks at risk.
4. **Incorporate Automation**: Set up workflows like automatic reminders or approvals to ensure the template is action-ready.

Step 2: Save as a Template

1. After finalizing your master sheet, click **File > Save as Template**.
2. Provide a descriptive name and a clear purpose for the template.

Step 3: Share Templates with Teams

1. Save templates in a shared workspace or folder.
2. Provide access to relevant team members to ensure uniform usage.

Implementing Standardized Processes

Beyond templates, standardizing workflows and processes ensures that all team members follow best practices consistently.

Key Areas for Process Standardization

1. **Task Assignment**: Define roles and responsibilities clearly within templates.
2. **Approval Workflows**: Establish consistent approval steps for key decisions.
3. **Reporting**: Use standardized dashboards and reports to track progress and share insights with stakeholders.
4. **Data Input**: Provide clear guidelines for data entry to maintain uniformity across sheets.

Best Practices for Standardization

1. Collaborate with Stakeholders

Involve team members in the creation of templates and processes to ensure they address actual needs and challenges.

2. Keep It Simple

Avoid overcomplicating templates or processes. Focus on essential elements that provide clarity and efficiency.

3. Test and Refine

Pilot new templates and processes with a small team before organization-wide implementation.

4. Train Your Team

Provide training sessions or resources to familiarize team members with standardized templates and workflows.

5. Regularly Review and Update

Revisit templates and processes periodically to ensure they remain relevant and effective.

Example: Standardizing a Project Tracking Template

Step 1: Key Elements to Include

- **Project Name**: Clearly labeled in the header.
- **Timeline**: Start and End Date columns with Gantt chart visualization.
- **Tasks**: Include columns for Task Name, Status, Priority, and Assigned To.
- **Dependencies**: Use Predecessor columns to link tasks.

Step 2: Add Automation

- Automate status updates based on task completion.
- Trigger reminders for upcoming deadlines.

Step 3: Save and Share

- Save as a template and distribute through a shared workspace.
- Provide guidelines for customization while maintaining core elements.

Troubleshooting Standardization Challenges

Problem: Inconsistent Template Usage

- **Solution**: Educate team members on the benefits of using standardized templates and processes.

Problem: Templates Not Meeting Team Needs

- **Solution**: Collect feedback from users and make iterative improvements.

Problem: Resistance to Change

- **Solution**: Highlight the time-saving benefits and improved efficiency that standardization provides.

Conclusion

Standardizing templates and processes in Smartsheet is a powerful strategy to improve efficiency, ensure consistency, and enhance collaboration. By implementing well-designed templates and streamlined workflows, your organization can focus on achieving project goals rather than reinventing the wheel for each new task.

Ensuring Data Security and Compliance

Data security and compliance are critical considerations in project management. Smartsheet provides robust features and practices to help organizations protect sensitive data and adhere to industry standards and regulatory requirements. This chapter explores how to leverage Smartsheet's capabilities to secure your data and maintain compliance.

Importance of Data Security and Compliance

Why It Matters

1. **Protecting Sensitive Information**: Safeguard proprietary and confidential data from breaches and unauthorized access.
2. **Maintaining Trust**: Build confidence with stakeholders by demonstrating a commitment to data security.
3. **Avoiding Legal Consequences**: Adhere to regulations such as GDPR, HIPAA, or SOC 2 to avoid fines and reputational damage.
4. **Supporting Business Continuity**: Reduce risks that could disrupt operations or compromise projects.

Smartsheet's Security Features

1. User Permissions and Access Control

Smartsheet offers granular control over who can view, edit, or share your sheets.

- **Roles and Permissions**: Assign roles such as Admin, Editor, or Viewer to team members.
- **Restricted Sharing**: Control whether users can share sheets or access data externally.
- **Enterprise Permissions**: For organizations, Smartsheet Enterprise allows centralized management of user access.

2. Two-Factor Authentication (2FA)

- Require 2FA for all users to add an extra layer of protection.
- Users must verify their identity using a secondary device when logging in.

3. Encryption

Smartsheet encrypts data both at rest and in transit, using advanced encryption protocols to secure information.

4. Audit Logs and Monitoring

Track user activity, including:

- Changes to sheets.
- Sharing activities.
- Logins and access attempts.

5. Custom Security Policies

- Implement password complexity and expiration rules.
- Restrict access by IP address or geographical location.

Ensuring Regulatory Compliance

Common Regulatory Standards

1. **GDPR (General Data Protection Regulation)**: Protects data privacy for EU citizens.
2. **HIPAA (Health Insurance Portability and Accountability Act)**: Ensures data security for healthcare organizations.
3. **SOC 2 (Service Organization Control 2)**: Focuses on data protection for service providers.

Smartsheet's Compliance Certifications

Smartsheet complies with industry standards and regulations, offering tools and guidance to help organizations meet requirements.

- **Trust Center**: Visit the Smartsheet Trust Center for up-to-date certifications and compliance details.
- **Data Residency**: For global organizations, Smartsheet supports data residency to store data in specific regions.

Best Practices for Data Security in Smartsheet

1. Implement Role-Based Access Control (RBAC)

- Assign roles based on the principle of least privilege.
- Limit access to only what users need to perform their tasks.

2. Use Secure Sharing Practices

- Share sheets with specific individuals instead of broadly sharing links.
- Require recipients to log in before accessing shared content.

3. Enable Two-Factor Authentication (2FA)

- Mandate 2FA for all users, including external collaborators.

4. Regularly Review Permissions

- Periodically audit access permissions to ensure they remain appropriate.
- Remove access for users who no longer need it.

5. Monitor and Respond to Activity Logs

- Use audit logs to detect unusual or unauthorized activity.
- Investigate and address incidents promptly.

6. Back Up Critical Data

- Export essential data and reports regularly for offline backups.
- Store backups securely to prevent loss in case of unforeseen incidents.

Troubleshooting Security and Compliance Challenges

Problem: Unauthorized Access

Solution: Review and tighten sharing permissions. Ensure 2FA is enabled for all users.

Problem: Inconsistent Application of Policies

Solution: Provide training on security practices and establish clear organizational policies.

Problem: Lack of Awareness Among Team Members

Solution: Conduct regular workshops or share resources to educate users on Smartsheet security features.

Case Study: Ensuring Compliance in a Healthcare Project

Scenario

A healthcare provider needed a Smartsheet solution for project tracking while complying with HIPAA requirements.

Solution

1. **Configured Permissions**: Restricted access to authorized team members only.
2. **Enabled Audit Logs**: Monitored all access and changes to ensure data integrity.
3. **Applied Encryption**: Ensured sensitive patient data was encrypted both at rest and in transit.
4. **Conducted Training**: Trained the team on HIPAA-compliant practices in Smartsheet.

Outcome

The organization successfully implemented Smartsheet to manage projects without compromising data security or compliance.

Conclusion

Smartsheet provides powerful tools to help organizations secure their data and meet regulatory requirements. By leveraging built-in security features and following best practices, you can protect sensitive information, ensure compliance, and maintain the trust of stakeholders.

Common Pitfalls and How to Avoid Them

As powerful as Smartsheet is, users often encounter challenges that can hinder productivity and project success. This chapter highlights common pitfalls, their impact, and practical solutions to overcome them, ensuring smooth and efficient use of Smartsheet in your projects.

1. Poorly Structured Sheets

The Pitfall

- Overloading sheets with excessive data, making them difficult to navigate.
- Using inconsistent naming conventions or column structures.

Impact

- Reduced efficiency as users struggle to locate or interpret information.
- Increased likelihood of errors due to disorganization.

How to Avoid

- **Plan Before You Build**: Design sheets with a clear purpose and structure in mind.
- **Use Consistent Naming**: Establish naming conventions for columns, rows, and files.
- **Keep It Simple**: Avoid overcomplicating sheets; use separate sheets for unrelated data.

2. Ineffective Collaboration Practices

The Pitfall

- Lack of clear ownership or responsibilities.
- Overuse of notifications, causing "alert fatigue" among team members.

Impact

- Missed deadlines due to unclear accountability.
- Reduced team engagement and responsiveness.

How to Avoid

- **Assign Responsibilities**: Use Smartsheet's "Assigned To" column to clarify ownership.
- **Tailor Notifications**: Configure alert rules carefully to avoid unnecessary updates.
- **Utilize Comments**: Collaborate effectively using row-specific comments for context.

3. Ignoring Automation Opportunities

The Pitfall

- Manually handling repetitive tasks, such as sending reminders or tracking updates.

Impact

- Wasted time on routine activities.
- Increased risk of human error.

How to Avoid

- **Explore Automation Features**: Use Smartsheet's automation workflows to handle reminders, approvals, and status updates.
- **Standardize Processes**: Develop templates with pre-built automations for common workflows.

---

4. Mismanaging Permissions

The Pitfall

- Granting overly broad access to sheets.
- Neglecting to revoke access for former collaborators.

Impact

- Risk of unauthorized edits or data breaches.
- Loss of data integrity due to untracked changes.

How to Avoid

- **Use Granular Permissions**: Assign specific roles (Admin, Editor, Viewer) based on user needs.
- **Review Access Regularly**: Conduct periodic audits of permissions to ensure they remain appropriate.

---

5. Overlooking Data Validation

The Pitfall

- Allowing unrestricted input in key fields, leading to inconsistent or inaccurate data.

Impact

- Difficulty analyzing data due to inconsistencies.
- Errors in reports or dashboards.

How to Avoid

- **Use Dropdowns**: Create predefined options for fields like status or priority.
- **Apply Conditional Formatting**: Highlight anomalies or invalid entries for quick identification.

---

6. Lack of Training and Onboarding

The Pitfall

- Team members are unfamiliar with Smartsheet features and best practices.

Impact

- Slow adoption and underutilization of the platform.
- Frustration among users, reducing productivity.

How to Avoid

- **Provide Training Resources**: Share guides, tutorials, and videos with new users.
- **Leverage Smartsheet University**: Encourage team members to explore Smartsheet's online learning platform.
- **Conduct Hands-On Workshops**: Host sessions to demonstrate real-world applications of Smartsheet.

7. Not Using Reports and Dashboards

The Pitfall

- Relying solely on raw data in sheets instead of summarizing key information.

Impact

- Inefficient reporting processes and difficulty providing stakeholders with insights.

How to Avoid

- **Create Custom Reports**: Use reports to extract and present relevant data for stakeholders.
- **Build Dashboards**: Summarize metrics visually for easier consumption.

8. Failing to Backup Data

The Pitfall

- Assuming Smartsheet's cloud storage is sufficient without regular backups.

Impact

- Risk of losing critical data in case of accidental deletions or unexpected issues.

How to Avoid

- **Schedule Regular Exports**: Export important sheets and reports as Excel or PDF files.
- **Use Third-Party Integrations**: Leverage tools like Zapier to automate backups to external storage.

9. Overcomplicating Automations

The Pitfall

- Creating overly complex workflows that are difficult to troubleshoot or manage.

Impact

- Automations fail to run as intended, causing delays or errors.

How to Avoid

- **Test Incrementally**: Build and test workflows step by step.
- **Keep It Simple**: Avoid chaining too many conditions or actions in a single automation.

10. Neglecting Regular Maintenance

The Pitfall

- Failing to update sheets, templates, or workflows as project needs evolve.

Impact

- Inefficiencies due to outdated processes.
- Loss of relevance in dashboards and reports.

How to Avoid

- **Schedule Periodic Reviews**: Review and update sheets, templates, and workflows regularly.
- **Involve Key Stakeholders**: Gather feedback to ensure updates align with current needs.

Conclusion

By addressing these common pitfalls proactively, you can maximize the value of Smartsheet and avoid unnecessary setbacks. The key is to combine strategic planning with ongoing education and maintenance, empowering your team to use Smartsheet effectively and efficiently.

Tips for Ongoing Improvement

Continuous improvement is vital for maximizing the value of Smartsheet in your project management workflows. By adopting a mindset of ongoing learning and refinement, you can ensure your processes remain efficient, scalable, and aligned with evolving project needs. This chapter outlines actionable strategies to help you and your team achieve ongoing success with Smartsheet.

1. Regularly Review and Update Templates

Why It Matters

Templates save time and ensure consistency. However, outdated templates can hinder efficiency and fail to address current project requirements.

Action Steps

- **Schedule Reviews**: Periodically evaluate templates to ensure they reflect your team's latest needs and best practices.
- **Incorporate Feedback**: Gather input from team members to identify areas for improvement.
- **Streamline**: Eliminate unnecessary fields or steps that add complexity without value.

2. Embrace Advanced Features

Why It Matters

Underutilizing Smartsheet's advanced features can limit your ability to automate tasks, analyze data, and manage projects effectively.

Action Steps

- **Explore New Features**: Stay updated on Smartsheet's latest capabilities by reviewing release notes and tutorials.
- **Experiment with Automations**: Test automation workflows to reduce manual tasks and enhance consistency.
- **Leverage Dashboards**: Build interactive dashboards to visualize key metrics and trends.

3. Foster a Culture of Collaboration

Why It Matters

A collaborative environment ensures everyone is aligned and actively contributing to project goals.

Action Steps

- **Set Clear Roles**: Use Smartsheet's "Assigned To" field and permissions to define responsibilities.
- **Encourage Real-Time Updates**: Use collaboration features like comments and notifications to keep everyone informed.
- **Promote Transparency**: Share dashboards and reports with stakeholders for enhanced visibility.

4. Invest in Training and Development

Why It Matters

Smartsheet's potential is fully realized when all team members are confident in using its features effectively.

Action Steps

- **Onboard New Users**: Provide a structured training program for new team members.
- **Host Regular Workshops**: Conduct periodic sessions to showcase tips, tricks, and advanced techniques.
- **Utilize Smartsheet Resources**: Encourage the use of Smartsheet University, webinars, and forums.

---

5. Monitor Key Metrics

Why It Matters

Tracking performance metrics helps identify inefficiencies and opportunities for improvement.

Action Steps

- **Define KPIs**: Identify the key performance indicators most relevant to your projects.
- **Automate Reporting**: Use Smartsheet's reporting features to generate regular updates automatically.
- **Analyze Trends**: Look for patterns that indicate recurring challenges or successes.

---

6. Simplify and Standardize

Why It Matters

Overly complex workflows and inconsistent practices can lead to confusion and inefficiency.

Action Steps

- **Audit Workflows**: Review existing processes to eliminate redundancies and unnecessary steps.
- **Use Standard Formats**: Create uniform structures for sheets, reports, and dashboards.
- **Consolidate Data**: Minimize duplication by linking related data across sheets instead of creating new ones.

---

7. Stay Informed on Industry Trends

Why It Matters

Project management best practices and tools evolve rapidly. Staying informed ensures your workflows remain relevant.

Action Steps

- **Follow Thought Leaders**: Subscribe to blogs, podcasts, or industry publications focused on project management.
- **Participate in Webinars**: Attend sessions hosted by Smartsheet or other experts in the field.

- **Network**: Join online communities or forums to share insights and learn from others' experiences.

---

8. Conduct Regular Check-Ins

Why It Matters

Frequent evaluations ensure your team remains aligned and any challenges are addressed promptly.

Action Steps

- **Host Retrospectives**: After major milestones or projects, discuss what worked well and areas for improvement.
- **Set Improvement Goals**: Identify specific objectives to enhance processes or workflows.
- **Document Changes**: Keep a record of updates for future reference and transparency.

---

9. Build a Knowledge Base

Why It Matters

A centralized repository of resources ensures team members can access information quickly and efficiently.

Action Steps

- **Create Documentation**: Develop guides for common tasks, troubleshooting, and best practices.
- **Organize Resources**: Use Smartsheet's attachments or a dedicated knowledge management tool.
- **Update Regularly**: Ensure the knowledge base remains relevant by reviewing and revising content.

---

10. Solicit Feedback Continuously

Why It Matters

Feedback from users is invaluable for identifying issues and uncovering opportunities for improvement.

Action Steps

- **Use Surveys**: Periodically survey team members to gather input on Smartsheet usage and workflows.
- **Encourage Open Communication**: Create an environment where team members feel comfortable sharing ideas.
- **Act on Suggestions**: Demonstrate responsiveness by implementing feasible recommendations.

Conclusion

Ongoing improvement in Smartsheet isn't a one-time effort—it's a continuous process that evolves with your team's needs and goals. By adopting these strategies, you can optimize your workflows, foster collaboration, and maintain peak efficiency in your project management endeavors.

Section 12:
Real-World Applications

Case Study: Marketing Campaign Management

In today's fast-paced marketing environment, teams need tools that can centralize planning, streamline execution, and ensure campaigns deliver measurable results. Smartsheet's versatility makes it an excellent choice for managing marketing campaigns, from initial strategy development to post-campaign reporting. This chapter delves into a real-world case study that illustrates how Smartsheet can empower marketing teams to succeed.

Overview of the Marketing Campaign

Objective: Launch a multi-channel product awareness campaign to drive engagement and lead generation for a new product.
Duration: Three months.
Key Channels: Social media, email marketing, paid advertisements, and events.
Team Composition: Marketing managers, designers, copywriters, and external vendors.

Challenges Faced Before Using Smartsheet

1. **Disjointed Communication**: With emails, spreadsheets, and separate tools in play, the team struggled to maintain alignment.
2. **Missed Deadlines**: Lack of real-time updates led to missed deadlines and last-minute scrambles.
3. **Ineffective Tracking**: Difficulty consolidating progress from multiple channels resulted in incomplete campaign insights.

Solution: Adopting Smartsheet

The marketing team implemented Smartsheet as their centralized campaign management tool. Key features included task tracking, calendar views, and dashboards for performance analytics.

Smartsheet Implementation

1. Campaign Planning

- **Master Sheet Setup**:
  The team created a master sheet to map the campaign timeline, assign responsibilities, and define milestones.
    - Columns: Task Name, Owner, Due Date, Status, Priority, Notes.
    - Rows: Individual campaign tasks segmented by channel (e.g., social media, email marketing).
    - Conditional Formatting: Highlighted overdue tasks in red and upcoming deadlines in yellow.

- **Collaborative Brainstorming**:
  Using Smartsheet's comments and attachments, team members shared ideas and uploaded reference materials directly to tasks.

---

2. Task Management and Scheduling

- **Automation Rules**:
  - Alerts for pending approvals and reminders for upcoming deadlines were automated.
  - Dependency management ensured tasks were completed in the correct sequence (e.g., ad creative finalized before launching campaigns).
- **Calendar View**:
  The team utilized Smartsheet's calendar view to visualize deadlines and adjust schedules to avoid conflicts.

---

3. Real-Time Collaboration

- **Team Coordination**:
  Team members updated task statuses directly in Smartsheet, ensuring everyone was aware of progress in real time.
- **External Vendor Collaboration**:
  Vendors were given limited access to relevant sheets, allowing them to upload deliverables and communicate without needing additional tools.

---

4. Campaign Performance Tracking

- **Custom Dashboards**:
  Dashboards were created to monitor campaign KPIs, such as click-through rates, engagement metrics, and lead generation figures.
  - Widgets: Chart for social media engagement, KPI tracker for email open rates, and graphs for ad performance.
- **Reporting**:
  Weekly automated reports were sent to stakeholders, summarizing key achievements and highlighting bottlenecks.

Results Achieved

1. **Improved Efficiency**:
   The team completed the campaign on time, with fewer delays compared to previous campaigns.
2. **Enhanced Collaboration**:
   Centralized communication reduced email clutter and improved coordination among team members and vendors.
3. **Data-Driven Decisions**:
   Real-time tracking and reporting enabled the team to optimize campaign elements, such as reallocating budget to higher-performing channels.
4. **Measurable Success**:
   The campaign exceeded its goals, achieving a 20% higher lead generation rate and 15% greater engagement compared to previous campaigns.

Best Practices for Marketing Campaigns in Smartsheet

1. **Define Clear Roles**: Assign specific owners to tasks and ensure accountability.
2. **Use Templates**: Save campaign structures as templates to reduce setup time for future campaigns.
3. **Monitor Progress Regularly**: Use dashboards to track KPIs and address issues as they arise.
4. **Leverage Automation**: Minimize manual follow-ups with automated reminders and alerts.
5. **Maintain Flexibility**: Adjust plans dynamically based on real-time performance data.

Conclusion

This case study demonstrates how Smartsheet can transform marketing campaign management. By centralizing workflows, enabling real-time collaboration, and providing actionable insights, Smartsheet helps teams achieve their objectives efficiently and effectively.

Case Study: IT and Software Development Projects

In the fast-paced world of IT and software development, managing complex workflows, multiple stakeholders, and evolving priorities is a significant challenge. Smartsheet provides a flexible and powerful platform to help IT teams streamline project management, from planning and execution to tracking and reporting. This chapter explores a real-world case study of how an IT organization used Smartsheet to manage a software development project effectively.

Project Overview

Objective: Develop and deploy a customer relationship management (CRM) software for a mid-sized enterprise within six months.
Scope: The project included requirements gathering, design, development, testing, and deployment phases.
Team Composition: Project managers, software developers, quality assurance (QA) testers, and client representatives.

Challenges Faced Before Using Smartsheet

1. **Fragmented Communication**: Team updates and documentation were scattered across multiple tools, leading to information silos.
2. **Inefficient Task Tracking**: Manual tracking methods made it difficult to monitor progress and identify bottlenecks.
3. **Unclear Dependencies**: A lack of visibility into task dependencies caused delays during critical phases.

Solution: Implementing Smartsheet

The IT team adopted Smartsheet to address these challenges and centralize their project management efforts. They leveraged Smartsheet's advanced features, including Gantt charts, automated workflows, and real-time dashboards.

Smartsheet Implementation

1. Project Planning

- **Master Project Sheet**:
  A master sheet was created to track all project tasks across phases. Key columns included:
    - Task Name
    - Owner
    - Start Date and Due Date
    - Dependencies
    - Status
    - Priority
- **Requirements Gathering Phase**:
  The team used Smartsheet's grid view to document client requirements, assign responsibilities, and set deadlines for approval.

- ○ Client representatives were added as collaborators to provide feedback directly in Smartsheet.

---

2. Task Management and Tracking

- **Gantt Chart for Dependencies**:
  The Gantt view helped visualize task dependencies and identify potential scheduling conflicts.
  - ○ Dependencies such as "Design Approval" preceding "Development Start" were clearly outlined.
- **Sprint Management**:
  For the development phase, tasks were organized into sprints. Each sprint was managed using Smartsheet's card view, offering a Kanban-style interface to track progress.

---

3. Collaboration and Communication

- **Centralized Updates**:
  Team members updated task statuses directly in Smartsheet, ensuring transparency across the project.
  - ○ Notifications and automated reminders were set up to keep stakeholders informed about upcoming deadlines.
- **Document Sharing**:
  Technical specifications, wireframes, and test cases were uploaded as attachments within relevant tasks for easy access.

---

4. Quality Assurance and Testing

- **Bug Tracking**:
  A separate sheet was created to track bugs identified during testing. Columns included Bug ID, Severity, Assigned Developer, Status, and Resolution Date.
- **Automated Notifications**:
  Developers received instant notifications when bugs were assigned to them, accelerating the resolution process.

---

5. Reporting and Dashboards

- **Custom Dashboards**:
  A project dashboard provided a real-time view of progress, highlighting key metrics such as:
  - ○ Tasks Completed vs. Pending
  - ○ Sprint Velocity
  - ○ Milestones Achieved
- **Weekly Reports**:
  Automated reports summarizing project status were sent to stakeholders, ensuring they remained informed throughout the development cycle.

Results Achieved

1. **Improved Efficiency**:
   The team completed the project on time, with fewer delays and a streamlined workflow.
2. **Enhanced Collaboration**:
   Centralized communication reduced misunderstandings and improved coordination among team members and stakeholders.
3. **Higher Quality Deliverables**:
   Comprehensive bug tracking and timely resolutions ensured a smoother deployment with minimal post-launch issues.
4. **Data-Driven Decisions**:
   Real-time dashboards provided actionable insights, enabling proactive issue resolution and better resource allocation.

Key Takeaways

- **Define Dependencies Early**: Use Gantt charts to ensure clear visibility into task dependencies and avoid bottlenecks.
- **Adopt Agile Principles**: Organize tasks into sprints and track progress using Kanban-style card views for iterative development.
- **Leverage Automation**: Set up notifications and reminders to minimize manual follow-ups and keep the team on track.
- **Monitor Metrics Regularly**: Use dashboards to track key performance indicators and adjust strategies as needed.

Conclusion

This case study illustrates how Smartsheet can transform the management of IT and software development projects. By centralizing workflows, fostering collaboration, and providing real-time insights, Smartsheet enables teams to deliver high-quality solutions on time and within budget.

Case Study: Event and Conference Planning

Planning events and conferences is a multifaceted endeavor involving multiple stakeholders, tight deadlines, and detailed logistics. Smartsheet serves as an indispensable tool to manage the complexity of such projects, ensuring all elements are coordinated efficiently. This chapter explores a case study of how a professional event planning team utilized Smartsheet to organize a large-scale conference successfully.

Project Overview

Event Name: Annual Business Innovation Summit
Objective: Host a conference for 500 participants, featuring keynote speakers, breakout sessions, and networking opportunities.
Scope: Venue selection, attendee registration, speaker coordination, marketing, and on-site execution.
Team Composition: Event manager, logistics coordinator, marketing team, and vendor representatives.

Challenges Before Using Smartsheet

1. **Disjointed Processes**: Various aspects of event planning, such as budgeting, marketing, and scheduling, were managed in separate tools.
2. **Limited Visibility**: The team lacked a centralized view of task statuses, leading to miscommunication and delays.
3. **Last-Minute Changes**: Adjustments to the schedule or vendor agreements were difficult to communicate effectively.

Solution: Implementing Smartsheet

The event planning team adopted Smartsheet to centralize their workflows, improve collaboration, and streamline communication. Key features such as templates, dashboards, and automation were leveraged for seamless execution.

Smartsheet Implementation

1. Initial Planning and Setup

- **Event Planning Template**:
  The team used Smartsheet's event planning template as a foundation, customizing it to include columns for Task Name, Owner, Status, Start Date, Due Date, and Priority.
- **Budget Tracking**:
  A separate sheet was created for the budget, categorizing expenses into venue costs, marketing, catering, speaker fees, and miscellaneous. The budget sheet included real-time updates on allocated versus actual expenses.

2. Managing Tasks and Milestones

- **Task Assignment**:
  Tasks such as venue booking, attendee outreach, and speaker arrangements were assigned to specific team members with clear deadlines.
- **Milestone Tracking**:
  Milestones like "Venue Contract Signed" and "Keynote Speaker Confirmed" were highlighted in the Gantt chart view for easy tracking.

---

3. Collaboration and Communication

- **Stakeholder Involvement**:
  External stakeholders, including vendors and sponsors, were added as collaborators with restricted access, allowing them to view and update relevant tasks.
- **Commenting and File Sharing**:
  Team members used Smartsheet's comment feature to discuss task-specific updates, while contracts and promotional materials were uploaded as attachments.

---

4. Automation for Efficiency

- **Reminders and Notifications**:
  Automated reminders were set up for upcoming deadlines, ensuring tasks like catering confirmations were completed on time.
- **Change Requests**:
  An automated workflow was implemented for change requests, streamlining approvals for schedule adjustments or additional budget allocations.

---

5. Real-Time Dashboards and Reporting

- **Event Dashboard**:
  A dashboard provided an overview of the event's progress, including:
  - Task completion percentage
  - Budget utilization
  - Registration numbers
- **Daily Status Reports**:
  Automated reports were sent daily to the event manager, summarizing pending tasks, milestones achieved, and potential risks.

Execution and Results

- **Smooth Event Execution**:
  On the day of the event, the team used Smartsheet to monitor on-site logistics, including check-in processes, session schedules, and vendor coordination.
- **Quick Adjustments**:
  When a speaker canceled last-minute, Smartsheet facilitated rapid updates to the agenda, notifying all stakeholders of the change immediately.
- **Post-Event Analysis**:
  After the event, Smartsheet was used to collect attendee feedback and analyze key metrics such as participant satisfaction and return on investment (ROI).

Key Takeaways

- **Centralized Management**: Smartsheet's templates and dashboards provide a comprehensive view of event planning activities, eliminating fragmented processes.
- **Enhanced Collaboration**: Features like comments and file sharing ensure seamless communication among internal teams and external stakeholders.
- **Proactive Risk Mitigation**: Automated reminders and workflows help teams stay ahead of deadlines and handle changes efficiently.
- **Measurable Outcomes**: Post-event reporting capabilities allow teams to assess performance and improve future events.

Conclusion

This case study demonstrates Smartsheet's versatility in managing the intricacies of event and conference planning. By integrating planning, tracking, and communication into one platform, teams can execute events with precision and confidence.

Lessons Learned from High-Performing Teams

High-performing teams consistently achieve exceptional results by leveraging effective strategies, tools, and collaboration techniques. Smartsheet plays a pivotal role in supporting such teams, enabling them to streamline workflows, foster communication, and maintain transparency. This chapter examines lessons learned from high-performing teams across various industries and highlights how Smartsheet contributes to their success.

Lesson 1: Centralize Information for Enhanced Visibility

Challenge

Many teams struggle with siloed information that hampers decision-making and progress tracking.

Solution with Smartsheet

High-performing teams centralize their data within Smartsheet to provide a single source of truth. Features such as customizable sheets, dashboards, and reports ensure that everyone has access to real-time information, reducing miscommunication and delays.

Key Takeaway

- Use **dashboards** to display project status, key performance indicators (KPIs), and progress metrics in one place.
- Maintain **centralized sheets** for tracking milestones, resource allocation, and task ownership.

Lesson 2: Prioritize Clear Communication and Collaboration

Challenge

Poor communication leads to missed deadlines, duplicated work, and frustration among team members.

Solution with Smartsheet

Smartsheet's collaboration features, such as commenting, notifications, and file sharing, enable teams to communicate effectively. High-performing teams use these tools to align stakeholders, document decisions, and ensure transparency.

Key Takeaway

- Leverage **comments and mentions** to facilitate task-specific discussions.
- Enable **automated alerts** to notify team members of updates or changes.

Lesson 3: Automate Repetitive Tasks to Save Time

Challenge

Manual processes slow down productivity and increase the risk of errors.

Solution with Smartsheet

High-performing teams utilize Smartsheet's automation capabilities to streamline workflows. Automated reminders, approvals, and data transfers free up time for strategic activities.

Key Takeaway

- Create **workflows** to automate routine actions, such as sending reminders or approving requests.
- Use **conditional paths** to handle complex scenarios with multiple dependencies.

Lesson 4: Foster Accountability Through Transparency

Challenge

Unclear roles and responsibilities often result in missed tasks and unmet expectations.

Solution with Smartsheet

Smartsheet's visibility features help teams assign clear responsibilities and track task progress. By maintaining transparency, high-performing teams hold members accountable while fostering trust and collaboration.

Key Takeaway

- Use **task ownership fields** to assign specific roles to team members.
- Regularly update **status columns** to track progress and address issues proactively.

Lesson 5: Monitor and Adapt Based on Real-Time Data

Challenge

Static reports and delayed insights hinder a team's ability to adapt to changing circumstances.

Solution with Smartsheet

High-performing teams rely on real-time data from Smartsheet to monitor performance and make informed decisions. Features like live dashboards and dynamic reports provide actionable insights into project health.

Key Takeaway

- Use **real-time dashboards** to track project metrics and identify bottlenecks.
- Generate **custom reports** to focus on specific aspects of a project, such as overdue tasks or budget overruns.

Lesson 6: Standardize Processes for Consistency

Challenge

Inconsistent processes lead to confusion and inefficiencies across projects.

Solution with Smartsheet

High-performing teams standardize their workflows using Smartsheet templates, ensuring consistency in planning, execution, and reporting. Standardization minimizes errors and accelerates onboarding for new team members.

Key Takeaway

- Develop **custom templates** tailored to your team's unique needs.
- Use **predefined workflows** to replicate best practices across projects.

Lesson 7: Embrace Continuous Improvement

Challenge

Stagnation in processes and tools can hinder a team's ability to scale and adapt.

Solution with Smartsheet

High-performing teams regularly review their workflows, gather feedback, and implement improvements. Smartsheet's flexibility allows teams to experiment with new features and refine processes over time.

Key Takeaway

- Conduct **post-mortem analyses** after each project to identify lessons learned.
- Use **Smartsheet Labs** and integrations to explore innovative solutions and extend functionality.

Real-World Example: High-Performing Marketing Team

Scenario

A global marketing team used Smartsheet to coordinate a multi-channel product launch. They implemented the following strategies:

- **Centralized Planning**: All campaign activities, including content creation, social media scheduling, and email marketing, were managed in a single Smartsheet.
- **Automated Approvals**: Creative assets were routed for approval using automated workflows.
- **Performance Dashboards**: Live dashboards displayed engagement metrics, enabling the team to pivot strategies in real time.

Outcome

The campaign achieved record-breaking results, with a 30% increase in engagement and a 25% reduction in turnaround time compared to previous launches.

Conclusion

High-performing teams demonstrate that success is built on a foundation of clear communication, efficient workflows, and continuous improvement. Smartsheet equips teams with the tools they need to overcome challenges, drive innovation, and achieve their goals. By applying these lessons, your team can unlock its full potential and deliver outstanding results.

Section 13:
The Road Ahead

Emerging Trends in Smartsheet and Project Management

The fields of project management and collaboration tools are evolving rapidly, with technological advancements and changing workplace dynamics shaping the future. Smartsheet, as a leader in work management solutions, continues to innovate, aligning with these trends to empower teams and organizations to achieve their goals more effectively. This chapter explores the emerging trends in Smartsheet and project management, offering insights into what lies ahead.

1. Increasing Adoption of AI and Automation

Overview

Artificial intelligence (AI) and automation are revolutionizing project management by enhancing efficiency, improving accuracy, and reducing manual workload.

Smartsheet's Role

- **Predictive Workflows**: Smartsheet is increasingly leveraging AI to predict project risks, forecast resource needs, and suggest corrective actions.
- **Automated Decision-Making**: Advanced automation capabilities are making it easier to implement complex workflows without extensive manual input.

Future Implications

- Teams will rely on AI-powered recommendations for task prioritization, resource allocation, and timeline adjustments.
- Automation will streamline repetitive tasks, enabling teams to focus on strategic activities.

2. Integration with Advanced Analytics Tools

Overview

Data-driven decision-making is becoming a cornerstone of effective project management. The ability to analyze and visualize complex data sets is critical.

Smartsheet's Role

- **Enhanced Dashboards**: Smartsheet continues to expand its dashboard capabilities, allowing for real-time data visualization and analysis.
- **Third-Party Analytics Integrations**: Seamless integration with tools like Tableau and Power BI provides deeper insights into project performance.

Future Implications

- Organizations will increasingly use integrated analytics to identify trends, measure KPIs, and predict project outcomes.
- Interactive dashboards will provide real-time updates, fostering informed decision-making.

3. Emphasis on Collaborative Workspaces

Overview

The rise of remote and hybrid work models has highlighted the need for collaborative platforms that enable seamless communication and teamwork.

Smartsheet's Role

- **Collaborative Ecosystems**: Smartsheet fosters collaboration through shared workspaces, real-time updates, and dynamic commenting.
- **Enhanced Communication Tools**: The platform is adopting advanced communication features to support distributed teams.

Future Implications

- Teams will work in virtual environments where collaboration tools are integrated with project management platforms.
- Real-time collaboration will reduce bottlenecks and enhance productivity across time zones.

4. Integration with Emerging Technologies

Overview

Emerging technologies like blockchain, augmented reality (AR), and virtual reality (VR) are finding applications in project management.

Smartsheet's Role

- **Blockchain for Security**: Future Smartsheet enhancements may include blockchain for secure data sharing and audit trails.
- **AR/VR for Planning**: Smartsheet Labs is exploring ways to integrate AR/VR for immersive project planning and visualization.

Future Implications

- Blockchain will improve trust and transparency in project management by creating immutable records.
- AR/VR will enable teams to visualize projects in 3D, enhancing understanding and stakeholder engagement.

5. Shift Towards Agile and Adaptive Methodologies

Overview

Agile project management is becoming the norm as teams prioritize flexibility, collaboration, and iterative progress.

Smartsheet's Role

- **Agile Tools**: Smartsheet's features, like Kanban boards and sprint tracking, support agile workflows.
- **Customizable Templates**: Teams can tailor Smartsheet templates to align with agile methodologies.

Future Implications

- Agile adoption will continue to grow, with tools like Smartsheet adapting to support hybrid approaches combining agile and traditional techniques.
- Teams will increasingly value tools that enable rapid adjustments and continuous delivery.

---

6. Focus on Sustainability and Social Responsibility

Overview

Organizations are prioritizing sustainability and ethical practices in their project planning and execution.

Smartsheet's Role

- **Environmental Metrics Tracking**: Smartsheet enables teams to monitor sustainability goals through customizable tracking sheets.
- **Social Responsibility Reporting**: The platform supports transparent reporting on corporate social responsibility (CSR) initiatives.

Future Implications

- Project management tools will integrate features for tracking environmental and social impact.
- Transparency in sustainability efforts will become a key differentiator for organizations.

---

7. Expanding Role of Low-Code and No-Code Platforms

Overview

The demand for tools that empower non-technical users to build and customize workflows is growing.

Smartsheet's Role

- **No-Code Workflows**: Smartsheet's automation tools allow users to create complex workflows without coding expertise.
- **App Development**: Smartsheet Labs offers low-code solutions for building custom applications.

Future Implications

- Teams will use no-code tools to rapidly prototype and deploy solutions.
- Customization will enable organizations to address unique project management needs efficiently.

---

8. Enhanced Mobile Capabilities

Overview

Mobile-first strategies are critical as teams increasingly work on the go.

Smartsheet's Role

- **Mobile App Enhancements**: Smartsheet's mobile app provides full functionality, including task updates, approvals, and collaboration.
- **Offline Access**: Future updates may include expanded offline capabilities for uninterrupted work.

Future Implications

- Mobile tools will become indispensable for remote and distributed teams.
- Enhanced mobile interfaces will improve accessibility and productivity.

Conclusion

Emerging trends in project management and collaboration are reshaping how teams approach their work. Smartsheet's commitment to innovation ensures it remains at the forefront of these changes, providing teams with the tools they need to adapt and excel. By staying informed about these trends and leveraging Smartsheet's capabilities, you can position your organization for long-term success in a rapidly evolving landscape.

Future Enhancements to Explore

As project management tools continue to evolve, Smartsheet remains committed to innovating and adapting to the changing needs of its users. Future enhancements to Smartsheet will likely focus on increasing efficiency, enabling deeper integrations, and offering more personalized and intelligent solutions. In this chapter, we'll explore potential enhancements Smartsheet could implement to further empower teams and drive project success.

1. Advanced AI-Driven Features

Predictive Analytics

Smartsheet could expand its use of artificial intelligence to predict project risks, resource needs, and timeline adjustments. These predictions could help managers proactively address potential issues.

AI-Powered Recommendations

Future enhancements may include AI-driven suggestions for task prioritization, workflow optimization, and resource allocation. This feature would be particularly useful for complex projects with competing priorities.

2. Deeper Integration Capabilities

Universal API Enhancements

Improved API functionality could make Smartsheet even more flexible, allowing organizations to connect it with niche tools and platforms specific to their industry.

Real-Time Integration Updates

Future integrations may include real-time data syncing across platforms, ensuring that changes made in Smartsheet are instantly reflected in connected tools like CRM systems or accounting software.

3. Enhanced Automation and Workflow Customization

Multi-Step Conditional Workflows

Smartsheet could expand its automation tools to allow for more complex, multi-step workflows based on various conditions, enabling greater flexibility and efficiency.

Workflow Templates

Pre-built workflow templates for common scenarios like budget approvals, onboarding, or procurement could save time and streamline operations.

4. More Powerful Reporting and Analytics

Dynamic KPI Dashboards

Future versions of Smartsheet might include dynamic dashboards that automatically adjust based on project progress or stakeholder requirements.

Customizable Data Visualizations

Enhanced reporting features could allow users to create fully customizable charts, graphs, and visualizations, catering to specific audience needs.

---

5. Broader Collaboration Tools

Integrated Video Conferencing

Smartsheet could introduce native video conferencing capabilities, eliminating the need to switch between platforms for virtual meetings and discussions.

Collaboration History

An improved version history feature could include detailed logs of changes, comments, and discussions, making it easier to track team contributions and decisions.

---

6. Mobile App Advancements

Offline Functionality

Future updates to the Smartsheet mobile app might include expanded offline capabilities, enabling users to make changes and updates that sync automatically once reconnected.

Voice Commands

Smartsheet could implement voice command features in its mobile app, allowing users to update tasks, add comments, or set reminders hands-free.

---

7. Augmented and Virtual Reality

Project Visualization

Using augmented reality (AR) or virtual reality (VR), Smartsheet could allow users to visualize project timelines, resource allocations, and dependencies in immersive 3D environments.

Training Simulations

AR/VR could be used to create interactive training modules, helping teams quickly learn how to use Smartsheet's advanced features.

---

8. Industry-Specific Solutions

Pre-Built Templates

Smartsheet could offer more industry-specific templates tailored for healthcare, education, manufacturing, and other sectors, streamlining setup for users.

Regulatory Compliance Features

Future enhancements might include built-in tools for tracking and ensuring compliance with industry-specific regulations, such as HIPAA for healthcare or GDPR for data privacy.

---

9. Greater Focus on Sustainability

Sustainability Tracking

Smartsheet could introduce features for tracking the environmental impact of projects, helping organizations meet their sustainability goals.

Eco-Friendly Workflows

Future updates might include tools for planning and executing eco-friendly workflows, such as reducing paper usage or optimizing resource allocation.

---

10. Enhanced Security and Privacy

Blockchain Integration

Blockchain technology could be used to secure project data, ensuring tamper-proof records and enhanced trust in data integrity.

Granular Permission Settings

Smartsheet could improve its permission settings, allowing for even more granular control over who can view, edit, or share specific data.

Conclusion

The future of Smartsheet is bright, with endless possibilities for innovation and enhancement. By staying ahead of emerging trends and continuously improving its features, Smartsheet ensures that it will remain a trusted tool for project management in an ever-evolving landscape.

As these potential enhancements become reality, users will gain even more power and flexibility, enabling them to tackle increasingly complex projects with confidence and success.

Key Takeaways and Next Steps

As we reach the conclusion of this journey through **Smartsheet Strategies: Driving Project Success**, it's time to distill the core principles and actionable insights from the book. This chapter provides a concise summary of the key takeaways and offers practical next steps to empower you to use Smartsheet effectively and confidently in your project management endeavors.

Key Takeaways

1. Smartsheet as a Flexible Project Management Tool

- Smartsheet is more than a project management platform—it's a dynamic, customizable tool that can adapt to the unique needs of your organization.
- Its user-friendly interface and cloud-based accessibility make it ideal for teams of any size or industry.

2. Foundation in Core Concepts

- Building a strong foundation in Smartsheet's core concepts—such as sheets, reports, dashboards, and automation—is critical to maximizing its potential.
- Familiarizing yourself with Smartsheet terminology and its basic navigation ensures a seamless experience.

3. Mastery of Essential Functions

- The ability to create and customize sheets, leverage pre-built templates, and utilize formulas is a game-changer for tracking and organizing your projects efficiently.
- Effective task management using Gantt charts, reminders, and alerts helps maintain project timelines and accountability.

4. Collaboration as a Pillar of Success

- Smartsheet excels in enabling collaboration, with features like real-time updates, comments, sharing options, and integrations with popular tools.
- Establishing clear roles, permissions, and streamlined communication channels enhances teamwork and ensures alignment.

5. Insights Through Reporting and Analytics

- Custom reports, interactive dashboards, and KPI tracking offer stakeholders the visibility they need to make informed decisions.
- Exporting and sharing reports in various formats ensures accessibility and ease of use.

6. Leveraging Integrations and Automation

- Connecting Smartsheet to third-party tools and building advanced workflows with conditional logic unlocks new levels of efficiency and innovation.
- Automations save time and reduce manual errors, allowing teams to focus on strategic tasks.

7. Best Practices for Long-Term Success

- Standardizing templates and processes ensures consistency across projects, while data security and compliance protect your organization's integrity.
- Regularly reviewing and updating workflows, sheets, and practices drives continuous improvement.

8. Industry-Specific Applications

- Smartsheet is versatile enough to manage a wide range of projects, from marketing campaigns to IT projects, event planning, and beyond.
- Case studies from high-performing teams highlight the value of tailored Smartsheet solutions in real-world scenarios.

Next Steps

1. Start with Small Wins

- Begin by implementing Smartsheet for a single project or team to familiarize yourself with its capabilities.
- Focus on mastering the basics—sheet creation, task tracking, and collaboration—before diving into advanced features.

2. Build a Knowledge Base

- Encourage your team to explore Smartsheet's Help Center, webinars, and community forums to learn from experts and peers.
- Create internal guides and training sessions to ensure team-wide adoption and proficiency.

3. Explore Advanced Features

- Experiment with advanced functionalities like automation, formulas, and dashboards to unlock the platform's full potential.
- Gradually integrate Smartsheet with other tools and software in your organization's ecosystem.

4. Iterate and Optimize

- Use Smartsheet's analytics and reporting tools to monitor your progress and identify areas for improvement.
- Regularly review and refine your workflows, templates, and practices based on team feedback and evolving project needs.

5. Stay Updated

- Smartsheet continuously evolves, introducing new features and enhancements. Stay informed by subscribing to product updates and attending Smartsheet events or webinars.
- Explore emerging trends and technologies, such as AI-driven analytics and integrations, to stay ahead in project management.

Conclusion

Smartsheet is a powerful ally in the quest for project success, offering tools and features to enhance planning, collaboration, tracking, and reporting. By adopting the strategies outlined in this book, you can harness Smartsheet's capabilities to streamline workflows, improve team efficiency, and achieve your project goals. Now, it's time to take the next step. Implement what you've learned, experiment with Smartsheet's possibilities, and refine your approach as you grow. Remember, project success isn't just about completing tasks—it's about creating value, fostering collaboration, and driving continuous improvement.

As you move forward, let Smartsheet be the backbone of your project management strategy, enabling you to turn ideas into actionable plans and plans into results. Here's to your success!

Appendices

Appendix A: Glossary of Smartsheet Terms

This glossary provides clear definitions of key terms and concepts in Smartsheet to help users navigate and fully utilize the platform. Use this as a quick reference guide as you work through your projects.

Active Cell

The currently selected cell within a sheet where data can be entered or edited.

Attachment

Files or links that can be added to rows, columns, or sheets for additional context or collaboration.

Automation

Rules created in Smartsheet to perform tasks automatically, such as sending reminders or updating data based on triggers.

Column Type

The format of a column that determines the type of data it holds (e.g., Text/Number, Dropdown, Date, Checkbox).

Conditional Formatting

A feature that applies specific formatting (like colors or icons) to cells based on defined criteria.

Dashboard

A visual and interactive display of critical data and metrics, often used for reporting or monitoring project status.

Dependencies

Relationships between tasks in a project, typically used in Gantt charts to represent task sequences (e.g., Finish-to-Start).

Dropdown List

A column type that provides predefined options for data entry, ensuring consistency.

Filter

A feature that displays only the rows that meet specified conditions, helping users focus on relevant data.

Form

A web-based input tool linked to a Smartsheet sheet, used for collecting data from users.

Gantt Chart

A visual timeline view that displays tasks and their durations, dependencies, and milestones.

Grid View

The default view in Smartsheet, displaying data in rows and columns similar to a spreadsheet.

Kanban Board

A project management tool within Smartsheet that visualizes tasks in a card-based layout, ideal for Agile workflows.

Milestone

A significant event or achievement in a project, typically marked on a Gantt chart without a duration.

Permissions

Settings that define the level of access users have to sheets, reports, and dashboards (e.g., Viewer, Editor, Admin).

Primary Column

The leftmost column in a sheet, used for identifying rows and organizing data.

Project Settings

Options in a project sheet that allow you to define dependencies, timelines, and resource management settings.

Publish

A feature that allows sheets, reports, or dashboards to be shared publicly or embedded into external platforms.

Recurring Task

A task that repeats on a set schedule, which can be managed with automations or manual updates.

Reminder

Automated or manual notifications sent to assigned users to ensure tasks are completed on time.

Report

A customizable view that consolidates data from multiple sheets based on specific criteria.

Resource Management

A feature that tracks team capacity and workload, ensuring efficient allocation of resources across projects.

Row Hierarchy

A structure that organizes rows into parent and child relationships, often used for grouping tasks or subtasks.

Sheet

The primary workspace in Smartsheet, where data, tasks, and project plans are managed.

Sights (Legacy Dashboards)

An older term for dashboards, still used in some legacy accounts.

Summary Fields

Customizable fields that provide a high-level overview of key metrics and data in a sheet or dashboard.

Template

Pre-built sheets or dashboards designed for specific use cases, which can be customized as needed.

Widget

An individual component of a dashboard, such as a chart, metric, report, or image.

Workspaces

Shared environments that group sheets, reports, and dashboards, allowing for organized collaboration.

Appendix B: Resource Links and Reference Materials

This appendix serves as a curated collection of resources, tools, and reference materials to help you deepen your understanding of Smartsheet and project management strategies. Use these links to expand your skills, stay updated on best practices, and explore advanced functionalities.

Official Smartsheet Resources

- **Smartsheet Help Center**
  Comprehensive guides and tutorials for using Smartsheet effectively.
  [Visit the Help Center] (https://help.smartsheet.com)
- **Smartsheet Learning Center**
  Free courses and certifications to build your Smartsheet expertise.
  [Visit the Learning Center] (https://www.smartsheet.com/learning-center)
- **Smartsheet Community**
  Connect with other users, share ideas, and get tips from experts.
  [Join the Community] (https://community.smartsheet.com)
- **Smartsheet Blog**
  Articles on project management, collaboration, and productivity trends.
  [Visit the Blog] (https://www.smartsheet.com/blog)
- **Smartsheet YouTube Channel**
  Video tutorials and webinars to help you learn Smartsheet faster.
  [Watch on YouTube] (https://www.youtube.com/smartsheet)

Third-Party Tools and Integrations

- **Zapier for Smartsheet**
  Automate workflows by connecting Smartsheet with other apps.
  [Learn More] (https://zapier.com/apps/smartsheet/integrations)
- **Smartsheet Add-Ons Marketplace**
  Explore extensions and tools to enhance Smartsheet functionality.
  [Visit the Marketplace] (https://www.smartsheet.com/marketplace)
- **Microsoft Office and Google Workspace Integrations**
  Guides for integrating Smartsheet with Excel, Word, Google Sheets, and more.
  [Office Integrations] (https://help.smartsheet.com/articles/1845225-microsoft-office-365)
  [Google Integrations] (https://help.smartsheet.com/articles/2047756-google-apps)
- **DocuSign for Smartsheet**
  Learn how to integrate e-signature capabilities with your workflows.
  [Learn More] (https://www.smartsheet.com/partners/docusign)

Project Management Frameworks

- **Agile Alliance**
  Resources for understanding and implementing Agile methodologies.
  [Visit Agile Alliance] (https://www.agilealliance.org)

- **PMI (Project Management Institute)**
  Guides, certifications, and resources for professional project management.
  [Visit PMI] (https://www.pmi.org)
- **Kanban Library**
  Free resources for mastering Kanban workflows.
  [Visit the Library] (https://kanbanize.com/kanban-resources)

Industry-Specific Resources

- **Marketing Project Templates**
  Smartsheet templates designed for marketing teams.
  [Download Templates] (https://www.smartsheet.com/marketing-templates)
- **IT and Software Development Tools**
  Resources tailored for IT teams and Agile developers.
  [Learn More] (https://www.smartsheet.com/it-project-management)
- **Event Management Solutions**
  Tools and case studies for managing events with Smartsheet.
  [Explore Solutions] (https://www.smartsheet.com/event-management)

General Productivity Tools

- **Trello vs. Smartsheet Comparison**
  Understand the differences and advantages of using Smartsheet.
  [Read the Guide] (https://www.smartsheet.com/blog/trello-vs-smartsheet)
- **Smartsheet Templates Gallery**
  A wide selection of free templates for various use cases.
  [Browse Templates] (https://www.smartsheet.com/templates)
- **Smartsheet Webinars and Events**
  Sign up for live or on-demand webinars to stay ahead.
  [View Webinars] (https://www.smartsheet.com/webinars)

Additional Reading

- **Books on Project Management**
  - *Making Things Happen: Mastering Project Management* by Scott Berkun
  - *Agile Project Management for Dummies* by Mark C. Layton
- **Books on Collaboration and Productivity**
  - *The Power of Collaboration* by The Deloitte Team
  - *Essentialism: The Disciplined Pursuit of Less* by Greg McKeown

---

This collection of resources ensures you have all the tools and materials needed to maximize your Smartsheet experience and advance your project management skills. Keep this appendix bookmarked for future reference!

Appendix C: Smartsheet Keyboard Shortcuts

Keyboard shortcuts are powerful tools that can dramatically improve your efficiency when working in Smartsheet. This appendix provides a comprehensive list of the most commonly used shortcuts to help you navigate, edit, and manage your sheets faster.

Navigation Shortcuts

- **Tab**: Move to the next cell.
- **Shift + Tab**: Move to the previous cell.
- **Arrow Keys**: Navigate up, down, left, or right within the sheet.
- **Ctrl + Home (Cmd + Home on Mac)**: Jump to the top-left corner of the sheet.
- **Ctrl + End (Cmd + End on Mac)**: Jump to the bottom-right corner of the sheet.

Editing Shortcuts

- **Enter**: Open the selected cell for editing.
- **Ctrl + Z (Cmd + Z on Mac)**: Undo the last action.
- **Ctrl + Y (Cmd + Y on Mac)**: Redo the last action.
- **Ctrl + C (Cmd + C on Mac)**: Copy the selected content.
- **Ctrl + V (Cmd + V on Mac)**: Paste the copied content.
- **Ctrl + X (Cmd + X on Mac)**: Cut the selected content.
- **Ctrl + D (Cmd + D on Mac)**: Duplicate the cell content to the row below.

Formatting Shortcuts

- **Ctrl + B (Cmd + B on Mac)**: Bold text.
- **Ctrl + I (Cmd + I on Mac)**: Italicize text.
- **Ctrl + U (Cmd + U on Mac)**: Underline text.
- **Alt + Enter (Option + Enter on Mac)**: Add a line break within a cell.

Row and Column Management

- **Ctrl + Spacebar (Cmd + Spacebar on Mac)**: Select the entire column.
- **Shift + Spacebar**: Select the entire row.
- **Ctrl + Shift + "+" (Cmd + Shift + "+" on Mac)**: Insert a new row.
- **Ctrl + "-" (Cmd + "-" on Mac)**: Delete the selected row or column.

View and Filter

- **Ctrl + F (Cmd + F on Mac)**: Open the Find and Replace dialog.
- **Ctrl + Shift + F (Cmd + Shift + F on Mac)**: Apply or clear filters.

- **Ctrl + Shift + L (Cmd + Shift + L on Mac)**: Toggle between collapsed and expanded views.

Gantt Chart View Shortcuts

- **Ctrl + Shift + G (Cmd + Shift + G on Mac)**: Open Gantt chart view.
- **Arrow Keys**: Navigate tasks in the Gantt chart.
- **Shift + Click**: Adjust dependencies between tasks.

Automation and Miscellaneous

- **Ctrl + Shift + A (Cmd + Shift + A on Mac)**: Access the Automations menu.
- **Ctrl + P (Cmd + P on Mac)**: Print the sheet.
- **F2**: Edit the selected cell without using the mouse.
- **Esc**: Cancel the current action or close a dialog box.

Customizing Shortcuts

For more advanced customization or additional shortcuts, visit the official Smartsheet Help Center. Smartsheet allows users to configure some shortcuts based on their preferences, especially for power users and enterprise teams.

[Explore Smartsheet Shortcut Options] (https://help.smartsheet.com)

This appendix provides quick access to the tools you need to boost productivity. Keep it handy as a reference while navigating and optimizing your Smartsheet workflows!

Conclusion

As we reach the conclusion of *Smartsheet Strategies: Driving Project Success*, it's essential to reflect on the journey we've taken through the depths of Smartsheet and its unparalleled potential in project management. This book has aimed to equip you with the knowledge and tools necessary to leverage Smartsheet to its fullest, transforming it from a simple work management tool into a cornerstone of your project success.

Summarizing the Core Lessons

1. **Foundation and Setup:**
   You've learned how to get started with Smartsheet, exploring its intuitive interface, terminology, and the steps to configure your account. A strong foundation ensures you can navigate the platform with confidence.
2. **Customization and Personalization:**
   Whether building sheets from scratch or customizing pre-built templates, you now understand how to tailor Smartsheet to meet your unique needs, ensuring every project is organized and easy to manage.
3. **Collaboration and Sharing:**
   Smartsheet's collaboration features allow seamless communication and teamwork. Real-time updates, comments, and controlled sharing ensure that every team member is aligned and informed.
4. **Advanced Workflows and Automations:**
   You've unlocked the potential of automation to reduce manual effort, improve efficiency, and focus on what truly matters—driving results.
5. **Data Visualization and Reporting:**
   By mastering interactive dashboards, detailed reporting, and KPI tracking, you can make data-driven decisions that keep projects on track and stakeholders satisfied.
6. **Best Practices and Real-World Applications:**
   From standardizing processes to exploring case studies, you've gained insights into how Smartsheet is applied across various industries and scenarios to achieve remarkable results.

The Road Ahead

The landscape of project management is ever-evolving, and Smartsheet is constantly innovating to meet the demands of modern teams. With trends like artificial intelligence, enhanced integrations, and expanded mobile capabilities, Smartsheet's potential will only continue to grow. Staying informed about these advancements will ensure that you remain at the forefront of effective project management.

Your Next Steps

1. **Put It into Practice:**
   Apply what you've learned in your own projects. Experiment with Smartsheet features and refine your workflows to match your team's unique goals.
2. **Educate and Empower Your Team:**
   Share your Smartsheet expertise with your colleagues. Collaboration is most effective when the entire team understands and utilizes the tools at their disposal.

3. **Stay Curious and Keep Learning:**
   Smartsheet regularly releases new features and updates. Explore the Smartsheet community, attend webinars, and dive into online resources to keep your skills sharp.

Gratitude and Final Thoughts

Thank you for choosing this book as your guide to mastering Smartsheet. Your dedication to improving your project management skills and driving success in your projects is commendable. With Smartsheet as your ally, you are well-equipped to tackle complex challenges, streamline workflows, and achieve excellence in your endeavors.

The possibilities with Smartsheet are vast—now it's your turn to harness them. Here's to your continued success in managing and executing projects with precision and impact!

Let's drive project success together.